DEDICATION

To David Augustus Embury, fellow Cornellian, whose classic 1948 work, *The Fine Art of Mixing Drinks*, offers this observation:

"The well-made cocktail is one of the most gracious of drinks. It pleases the senses. The shared delight of those who partake in common of this refreshing nectar breaks the ice of formal reserve. Taut nerves relax, taut muscles relax, tired eyes brighten, tongues loosen, friend-ships deepen — the whole world becomes a better place in which to live."

CARTE DU JOUR

PROLOGUE

"Of all the gin joints, in all the towns, in all the world...
she walks into mine."

— Humphrey Bogart
as Rick Blaine in *Casablanca* (1942)

Some things only happen in the movies. But the boozy backdrop in *Casablanca* was a lot like the real world in the 1940s. While Sasha, the "crazy Russian" bartender, mixed gin and champagne into elegant French 75s at fictional Rick's Café, real life bartenders were crafting intoxicating potions in urban nightclubs and civilized cocktail lounges all around the globe.

You may be "shocked, shocked" to learn that most cocktails owe their life to bootleg gin, the homemade swill of Prohibition-era America. First blended to mask the grim taste of illicit booze, cocktails emerged from our Noble Experiment as the embodiment of fashion and style. Having stood the test of time and taste, these concoctions have encouraged intelligent conversation, inspired artists, authors, and composers, and supplied good cheer to millions of elbow-benders. H.L. Mencken once described the cocktail as "the greatest of all contributions of the American way of life to the salvation of humanity."

For much of 20th century history, gin-based drinks, most notably the iconic Martini, held a monopoly on rituals of indulgence over our mahogany rostrums. Times change, and while the gin category may have been temporarily overshadowed by vodka's neutral palate and the malt pedigree of Scotch whisky, the re-emergence of cocktail craft has helped to restore the status of our most versatile of spirits. Engaging and complex, sophisticated and quirky, gin has become a vital component in the mixing cups of a new breed of artisan drinksmiths.

Compiling an honest compendium of honored establishments and their highest endeavors with the botanically-infused elixir required rigorous field work, counseled by W.C. Fields who never drank "anything stronger than gin before breakfast." Offered for your amenity is the guide to a journey around the upper echelon of the bartending profes-

1

sion in one-hundred-and-one recipes — exploratory gin-based concoctions developed with almost appalling care in the progressive cocktail laboratories of American "gin joints," often bringing methods and flourishes of the kitchen to the glass with fresh juices, muddled fruit, infused syrups, earthy spices, and leafy herbs. As these men and women zero in on gin's amazing mixing powers, they elevate the art of mixology to new heights. There's a ceremony, a theater to what they do, and the resulting pleasures are considerable.

With this volume as trusted companion, you'll be able to re-create their remarkable formulas with precision and authenticity. I hope each raised glass provides the beginning of a beautiful friendship.

Michael Turback
Citizen of the World

Gin-ealogy 101

In his 1941 classic, *Cocktail Guide and Ladies' Companion*, Crosby Gaige, theatrical producer and bon vivant, called gin the "universal stimulant of the million and the millionaire." There have been so many colorful legends attributed to the distilled spirit, it's almost a shame to spoil it all with the true story.

While there are more than one hundred botanical ingredients that may be used in the production of gin, an account necessarily begins with small, round, bluish-black berries — not true berries at all, but scales on the cones of prickly juniper bushes that look like berries — whose roots reach back into ancient history.

In Egypt, juniper was used in the embalming ritual, securing pharaohs for "eternal life," a fact confirmed by the discovery of mummies holding juniper berries in their dried hands. The resinous, pine/spruce aromatics of juniper were trusted by both Egyptians and Greeks to ward off infections and disease. In Greece, Olympic athletes soaked in hot baths of crushed juniper berries to increase their strength and stamina. During the outbreak of bubonic plague which killed a third of the European population in the 14th century, people wore masks filled with "antiseptic" juniper against exposure.

By the late 16th century, juniper berries had been proven effective as diuretic and carminative, and during this period a Dutch physician by the name of Sylvius de Bouve first infused a distillation of barley wine with the life essence of juniper as treatment for kidney infections. He found that curative properties in the berries transferred to the liquid, making it more agreeably ingested by his patients. The doctor called his remedy *eau de vie de genièvre* (French for juniper spirits), and while intended to rid the body of toxins, it fell into popular use as an alcoholic beverage.

Genièvre accompanied Dutch soldiers during their 80-year-long struggle for independence from Spain. Troops prepared to engage in battle with bravery-bolstering shots of the juniper-charged elixir, a practice that did not go unnoticed by their British comrades who called the drink "Dutch Courage."

It's astonishing to think, then, to realize how much a drink can contribute to the social upheaval of a country. As British soldiers returned from the war, they brought the taste for genièvre (a term the Brits shortened to "gin") along with them across the English Channel. Put the blame on good king William III, if you want — he encouraged unfettered production of gin by abolishing taxes and licensing fees. The working classes responded with mass public drunkenness, brawling, child neglect, and prostitution. By the 1720s, London was riddled with squalid shops selling cheap gin, inspiring colloquial expressions ("gin mills" and "gin joints") that survive to this day.

The Tippling Act reforms of 1751 marked the beginning of the end of "gin madness" in England, and although producers began an effort to make gin respectable, the spirit remained out of favor with upper classes until the era of Colonial rule. British soldiers stationed in the tropical colonies were required to swallow a daily dose of bitter quinine to ward off malarial fevers. Instead of taking the quinine with their troops at dawn, officers splashed gin into it, imbibing during what became a late afternoon ritual. It was the birth of the gin-and-tonic partnership and the introduction of the civilized cocktail hour. (Damned clever, those British).

The ascendance of gin in America did not occur until the "Great Drought" of Prohibition when bootleggers soaked juniper berry extract in bathtubs filled with raw alcohol. Crude synthetic or "bathtub" gins served in speakeasies inspired the uniquely American works of mischief called cocktails, disguising obnoxious hooch with flavorings from the likes of sodas, juices, cream, and sugar. Repeal in 1933 ended criminal manufacture, yet gin remained at the center of cocktail culture. By 1942, about the same time Rick Blaine was contemplating "all the gin joints" Ilsa Lund might have walked into, over 300 different gin-based cocktail recipes had been developed by the nation's bartenders, most notably a *pas de deux* called the Dry Martini.

The earliest Martinis were made with equivalent measures of gin and vermouth (also known as the Cornell Cocktail). Then, as the quality of gins improved, the gin-vermouth ratio expanded from 3-to-1 all the way to 15-to-1 and beyond. Ernest Hemingway called his preferred lubricant the "Montgomery Martini," inspired by Field Marshal Montgomery who supposedly refused to go into battle unless his numerical advantage was at least 15-to-1. Historian Bernard DeVoto called it "the supreme American gift to world culture," and in a manner shared by no other cocktail, the Martini became a symbol of success and the "American Dream."

From this history, the luxuriant spirit of multiple distillations has emerged in a variety of expressions, delivering layer upon layer of flavor to culture's evolving palate. London Dry can be produced anywhere, but to earn the name, the base spirit must be rectified to neutrality before being redistilled with predominant juniper and citrusy flavorings for which the drink is renowned. Plymouth is a more robust style, slightly fruity, and very aromatic. Old Tom (its name derived from a wooden plaque in the shape of an old tom cat outside a London gin mill) is the last remaining example of the lightly-sweetened gins that were popular in 18th-century England. Genever is the primordial Dutch style, distilled from a malted grain mash similar to the base used for whisky, and for the purpose of pouring cocktails, a separate product category.

Every generation edits history for its own tastes. The most recent chapter introduces small-batch gins from a new wave of cocky, young craft distillers. While styles of the moment often include a supporting cast of herbs, spices, and a Carmen Miranda basket of fruits and vegetables, juniper, in most instances, endures as the defining sensory profile — the seductive "nose" that fills the air when a fresh bottle of gin is opened.

Since each distiller has his own secret formula and no two gin brands are exactly alike, you are encouraged to experiment with new gins as well as the usual suspects to assure the most compatible makings to suit your taste, your full enjoyment of each sip.

So lift your glass and offer a toast to gin – invented by the Dutch, refined by the British, and glamorized by Americans. Borrowing the toast offered by *Casablanca*'s Rick Blaine, "Here's looking at you, kid."

Tools of the Trade

Boston Shaker

Dating all the way back to late 19th century "Beantown," the Boston shaker has been a fundamental tool behind the bar, and it remains the professional standard, pure and simple. The two-piece shaker consists of a stainless steel cup and mixing glass; the glass is used alone for stirring drinks with ice, and the two pieces are joined together for shaking ingredients with the cup fitting over the glass, creating a seal when gently tapped into place. (When making two drinks at once use less ice to make room in the shaker).

TIP: Shaking technique should result in a drink that's cold, yet undiluted, simultaneously blended and aerated. In The Thin Man, *William Powell instructs his bartender on the art of shaking: "The important thing is the rhythm. Always have rhythm in your shaking. Now a Manhattan you always shake to fox-trot time, a Bronx to two-step time, a dry Martini you always shake to waltz time."*

Hawthorne Strainer

The all-purpose strainer is a paddle-like, perforated metal device with a continuous coil of wire around its perimeter, ensuring a spillproof fit, compatible with the Boston shaker. For drinks that are shaken or stirred with ice and served neat or over new ice, the strainer is used to separate ice from the liquid.

TIP: Place your index finger over the handle to hold it firmly in place and strain the drink into the serving glass. To get the last drop, give the shaker a sharp twist as you return it to an upright position.

Fine-Mesh Strainer

Pouring from a Boston shaker with a Hawthorne strainer through a tea strainer or a fine mesh strainer is known as "double straining." This secondary filter removes smaller particles, froth, pulp, seeds, and other unwanted ingredients, insuring a clean, clear drink.

TIP: This tool is indispensable when mixing cocktails with herbs, such as mint or basil.

Jigger and Pony

Ingredients in proper cocktails must be measured to the fraction of an ounce. A stainless steel instrument with two opposing cones in an hourglass shape is recommended for precise, consistent calibration of liquids in the preparation of cocktails. The larger cone (jigger) typically holds 1 1/2 ounces while the smaller cone (pony) holds 3/4 ounce. With no need for the guesswork of free-pouring, cocktails will honor the recipe a skilled bartender labored to create. (In countries that use the metric system, the measures are usually 40 ml and 20 ml).

TIP: Charles H. Baker Jr. calls cocktail mixing "an exacting chemical art." Consider purchasing other jiggers for more specific measurements. Single jiggers come in iterations from a quarter of an ounce to two ounces.

Bar Spoon

Certain cocktails, particularly those made with spirits only, should always be stirred, chilling the drink without the undue aeration of shaking. Essential to stirring, the metal, long-handled bar spoon (for reaching the bottom of tall glasses) has a spiral handle (for easy twisting of the shaft) used to agitate or twirl ice through the ingredients and a spoon used for a teaspoon measure.

TIP: Hold the twisted shaft of the bar spoon between your thumb and first two fingers. Dunk the bar spoon into the glass and twirl the shaft back and forth and up and down in a fluid motion for 10 to 20 seconds to achieve the desired temperature.

Muddler

Similar to a pestle, the muddler is a blunt instrument used to mash and agitate herbs, fruits, or other solid ingredients in the bottom of a mixing glass, extracting flavors and aromatics. Most commonly made of hardwood, the muddler should be artfully weighted and teardrop-shaped, with a diameter of about 1 1/2 inches at the widest point and long enough to reach the bottom of mixing glasses. (The muddler of the moment is the "Pug," each piece hand-turned on a lathe by barman Chris Gallagher).

TIP: When muddling herbs to release essential oils, be gentle, avoiding the release of bitterness from the stems. For muddling fruit such as strawberries, cutting into small pieces makes them easier to work with.

Ice Tray

Oversize ice cubes help maintain the integrity of cocktails. A larger, thicker surface melts slower, so drinks stay colder longer and don't get watered down. Use larger molds to freeze distilled, purified, natural spring or bottled water, and keep the ice fresh by rotating in and out of the freezer.

TIP: A good drink is very cold. Keep your bottle of gin in the refrigerator and always chill glasses. To pre-chill, fill glasses to the brim with ice and water (soda water works best) and let them sit while you mix the drinks. Just before pouring drinks, discard the contents of each glass.

Bar Knives

Adding a garnish of citrus zest, twist, or peel "medallion" provides the finishing touch to many cocktails. A sharp paring knife and cutting board are basic requirements. In addition, the zester/channel knife combo uses small circular holes to zest the aromatic peel of citrus fruits (without grating into the bitter pith) and a blade that cuts a 1/4-inch wide strips of rind for spirals.

TIP: To liberate the wonderfully aromatic spray of essential oil over a drink, hold the peel horizontally about one inch above the surface, outer skin side facing downward. Gently but firmly twist one end clockwise and the other counterclockwise. Rub the outside of the peel around the rim of the glass so that any remaining oils adhere to the rim and drop into the drink.

Citrus Juicer

Always use fresh-squeezed lemons, limes, or oranges for more aromatic and fresher-tasting drinks. The hand-press citrus juicer provides small amounts of juice with a minimum of effort. Simply insert the halved fruit into the bowl of the squeezer and press down, using the top part to push the juice through the strainer. The bowl juicer is another way to easily juice citrus fruits and store small amounts of juice before adding it to a recipe.

TIP: To get the most juice yield out of your citrus, use fruits at room temperature. Roll the fruit with your palm on the kitchen countertop a few times before you juice.

Glassware

The proper glass for a cocktail may also be considered a tool. Glassware is available in a wide range of styles, sizes, and decorative motifs, and while fashion and presentation can heighten the imbibing experience, more basic criteria should be contemplated. Ideal for a straight-up cocktail, the shallow, curvaceous coupe encourages one to sip a drink rather than tossing it back in large gulps, and its stem allows a drinker to hold the glass without affecting the temperature; the wide bowl places the surface of the drink directly under the drinker's nose, ensuring that the aromatic element has the desired effect.

TIP: The coupe started life as a champagne glass, later adapted to holding cocktails in swanky, post-Prohibition nightclubs during the 1930s and 40s. The coupe is in vogue once again, both for its versatility as well as homage to the heyday of cocktail culture.

Fluid Measures and Equivalents

1 teaspoon = 5 ml
1 tablespoon = 15 ml
1 ounce = 30 ml
1 cup = 235 ml
1 quart = 950 ml

10 ml = 2 teaspoons
50 ml = 3 tablespoons
100 ml = 3 1/2 ounces
250 ml = 1 cup + 1 tablespoon
500 ml = 1 pint + 2 tablespoons

Making Simple Syrup

Many cocktail recipes call for simple syrup (or bar syrup) as a sweetener, often used to balance citric acid. The "recipe" couldn't be easier to execute: add one cup water into a pan, bring to a boil, then stir in 1 1/2 cups (or up to 2 cups) of plain granulated sugar. Turn the heat to low and stir continually until the sugar dissolves completely. Allow the syrup cool to room temperature, then pour into a clean glass jar and store in the refrigerator.

THE COCKTAILS THEMSELVES

DARKSIDE
ADAM BERNBACH
PROOF, WASHINGTON, DC

With a steady stir of the long cocktail spoon between his second and middle finger, Mr. Bernbach combines a botanical-forward gin with Barolo Chinato, an aromatic wine, aged in oak barrels with China Calissaya bark and alpine herbs. A dash or two of bitters adds concentrated flavors of anise and cherry to a "bar noir" apertivo, guaranteed to stimulate both appetite and conversation.

Ingredients:

2 1/4 ounces gin
3/4 ounce Barolo Chinato
2 dashes Peychaud's bitters
1 teaspoon spiced cherries*

Method:

Combine the gin, Chinato, and bitters in a mixing glass filled with ice. Stir to chill and strain into a pre-chilled coupe. Garnish with spiced cherries.

*Soak 1/2 cup dried sour cherries in a bath of 1 ounce cardamom and coriander-infused brandy, 1 ounce absinthe, and 2 ounces Barolo Chinato. Strain just before use.

Yield: 1 drink

GIN STING
LYDIA REISSMUELLER
TENDER BAR, PORTLAND, OR

"More than a vegetal variation on the Martini," says Ms. Reissmueller, "I think of this as alter-ego to the Mojito." A tincture of nettles pressed with mint leaves adds earthy, herbaceous notes and releases sweet, sensuous aromatics. It is said that Alexander the Great banned his soldiers from chewing on mint leaves, fearing that they would become sexually excited and unable to fight effectively.

Ingredients:

8 fresh mint leaves (plus 1 leaf for garnish)
1 teaspoon of nettles tincture
2 ounces gin
1/2 ounce dry vermouth
1/4 ounce honey syrup*
1/2 teaspoon grated lemon peel

Method:

Chop 8 mint leaves into small pieces. Place in a small bowl, add the nettles tincture and stir to combine. Place cheesecloth in a sieve and pour the mixture through, pressing down on the plant material to extract all liquid. Combine the herbal liquid, gin, vermouth, and honey syrup in a mixing glass filled with ice. Stir to chill and strain into an Old Fashioned tumbler over 1 large ice cube. Garnish with a single mint leaf and grated lemon peel.

*In a small saucepan, combine 1/2 cup honey, 1/4 cup water, and 2 tablespoons fresh lemon juice over medium heat, stirring occasionally until boiling. Continue to boil until the mixture is reduced by one-fourth. Cover and store in refrigerator until ready to use.

Yield: 1 drink

Hungarian Rhapsody No. 2
Lydia Reissmueller
Tender Bar, Portland, OR

Composer Franz Liszt was influenced by Hungarian folk music, with its unique gypsy scale, rhythmic spontaneity and direct, seductive expression. In Ms. Reissmueller's harmonic libation, gin provides the essential chord, while citrus and bitter chocolate notes of the herbal Zwack liqueur are amplified by the bitters and balanced by the bubbly, creamy soda. Suggested as a not-too-sweet dessert tipple.

Ingredients:

1 ounce gin
1 ounce Zwack liqueur
2 dashes orange bitters
2 dashes Fee Brothers Aztec Chocolate Cocktail Bitters
1 1/2 ounces Virgil's Cream Soda
1/2 orange wheel*
dark chocolate, grated

Method:

Combine the gin, Zwack, and bitters in a mixing glass filled with ice. Stir to chill and strain into a pre-chilled coupe. Add the cream soda and fill the glass with crushed ice. Place the orange wheel on top and sprinkle with the grated chocolate.

*Position a whole orange so that the ends are facing your right and left. Choose an end to start with and begin slicing off wheels. Cut so the orange wheels are thin, but firm. Cut wheels in half for garnishes.

Yield: 1 drink

BITTER ENEMY
SEAN THIBODEAUX
CLEVER, NEW ORLEANS, LA

French aperitif wine, Lillet Blanc, and St. Germain Liqueur are harmonious, complimentary companions to gin, supporting the piquant and complex bitter palate of a cocktail one may find appropriate at either end of a meal — to encourage appetite or aid digestion. Its name, Mr. Thibodeax explains, is derived from an old Scottish proverb: "False friends are worse than bitter enemies."

Ingredients:

1 1/2 ounces gin
1/2 ounce Lillet Blanc
1/2 ounce St. Germain Elderflower Liqueur
1/4 ounce clove simple syrup*
1/4 ounce fresh-squeezed lemon juice
4 to 5 drops Angostura bitters

Method:

Combine all ingredients with ice in a shaker. Shake vigorously and double strain into a pre-chilled coupe. Serve without garnish.

*In medium saucepan over medium heat, stir together 6 whole cloves, 1/2 cup water and 1/2 cup sugar until sugar dissolves. Slightly increase heat, simmer 5 minutes, stirring occasionally. Remove from heat and allow to cool down. Just before use, strain to remove the cloves.

Yield: 1 drink

THE AZTEC
SEAN THIBODEAUX
CLEVER, NEW ORLEANS, LA

The jalapeño pepper is named for the city of Jalapa in central Mexico, a region once dominated by the Aztec civilization. It provides both theme and heat to a cocktail informed by the "Martinez" (later morphed into the "Gin and It"), with tradition calling for sweet vermouth and orange bitters. "The heat is subtle," assures Mr. Thibodeaux. "There's no pain involved."

Ingredients:

2 ounces gin
1 ounce sweet vermouth
1/2 ounce jalapeño-infused Chartreuse (yellow)*
2 dashes orange bitters
orange peel medallion

Method:

Combine the gin, vermouth, infused Chartreuse, and bitters in a mixing glass filled with ice. Stir to chill and strain into a pre-chilled coupe. Squeeze orange peel over surface to express oils and drop into the cocktail.

*Using a gas-fired stove top, place a jalapeno pepper directly over the flame. Allow both sides to blacken and bubble up, about 1 minute. Peel off skin and remove seeds. Place the pepper and 1 cup of Chartreuse in a mason jar and set aside for 12 to 24 hours. Strain the pepper from the liquid using a cheese cloth or strainer and rebottle.

Yield: 1 drink

LOLITA
JERMAINE WHITEAD
BARRIO CAPITOL HILL, SEATTLE, WA

Vladimir Nabokov's literary classic inspired the fanciful notion. His protagonist, Humbert Humbert, always seems to have a bottle of gin nearby, and he expressively describes Lolita's skin as "apricot." Mr. Whitead's gin-based homage calls for a liqueur that combines a floral-scented eau-de-vie with the juice of apricots grown in the Danube River valley. Citrus and bitters bring balance and complexity to a master-piece of scene stealing.

Ingredients:

1 1/2 ounces gin
3/4 ounce Rothman & Winter Orchard Apricot Liqueur
1/2 ounce fresh-squeezed lemon juice
1 or 2 dashes Angostura bitters
1/4 ounce dry vermouth
lemon peel medallion

Method:

Combine the gin, apricot liqueur, lemon juice, bitters, and vermouth with ice in a shaker. Shake vigorously and double strain into a pre-chilled cocktail glass. Squeeze lemon peel over surface to express oils and drop into the cocktail.

Yield: 1 drink

GIN JUNKIE
ALEKO LILLY
BARRIO CAPITOL HILL, SEATTLE, WA

Mr. Lilly gives a brilliant account of his obsession with gin. Caraway-infused aquavit provides an intriguing counterpoint to the juniper flourish, with the citrusy notes of St. Germaine, aromatics of orange bitters, and sweetening properties of cactus-based agave adding additional layers of flavor and complexity. His ingredients fit together as smoothly as the pieces of a hand-cut jigsaw puzzle.

Ingredients:

1 1/2 ounces gin
1/2 ounce Linie Aquavit
1/4 ounce St. Germain Elderflower Liqueur
1/4 ounce agave nectar
2 dashes orange bitters
lemon peel medallion

Method:

Combine the gin, aquavit, elderflower liqueur, agave syrup, and bitters in a mixing glass filled with ice. Stir to chill and strain into a pre-chilled cocktail glass. Squeeze lemon peel over surface to express oils and drop into the cocktail.

Yield: 1 drink

Napoleon Complex

Stephen Shelton
Cin-Cin, Los Gatos, CA

"Imagination rules the world," declared Napoleon Bonaparte. It's with a delightful complexity and interplay of aromatics that Mr. Shelton's inventive formula captures the senses as well as the imagination. Fragrant lavender syrup supports the tantalizing bouquet of Lillet and the orchestra of botanicals of gin. A spot of the orange's sweet acidity balances texture and brightens the palate.

Ingredients:

1 1/2 ounces gin
3/4 ounce lavender syrup*
3/4 ounce Lillet Blanc
1/4 ounce fresh-squeezed orange juice
lemon peel medallion

Method:

Combine the gin, lavender syrup, Lillet, and orange juice with ice in a shaker. Shake vigorously and double strain into a pre-chilled cocktail glass. Squeeze lemon peel over surface to express oils and drop into the cocktail.

*Combine 3/4 cup water, 1/2 cup turbinado or unrefined sugar, 2 fresh lavender blossoms (or 1 teaspoon dried) and 1 fresh basil leaf in a saucepan, and bring to a boil. Remove from heat, cover and let cool. Strain and refrigerate.

Yield: 1 drink

BLOSSOM DEARIE
STEPHEN SHELTON
CIN-CIN, LOS GATOS, CA

Before dark purple elderberries ripen during late summer, the wild shrub produces clusters of small white or cream-colored flower blossoms. These blossoms, harvested in the French countryside, are distilled and blended with a small amount of citrus and natural cane sugar, resulting in a delicate liqueur with fresh floral aromas and flavor hints of pear, apricot and grapefruit zest. The easy confluence of St. Germaine with gin and herbaceous basil inspires a lively, aromatic summertime refreshment.

Ingredients:

6 to 8 fresh basil leaves
1 3/4 ounces gin
3/4 ounce St. Germain Elderflower Liqueur
fresh-squeezed juice of 1/2 lime
sparkling water
fresh basil flower, for garnish

Method:

Add basil leaves to a mixing glass and muddle gently while keeping the leaves intact. Fill the glass two-thirds full of ice cubes. Add gin, elderflower liqueur, and lime juice. Shake lightly and strain into a Collins glass filled with ice. Top with a splash of sparkling water and garnish with basil flower.

Yield: 1 drink

YERBA BUENA
STEPHEN SHELTON
CIN-CIN, LOS GATOS, CA

According to Mr. Shelton, "this one's for the Gimlet drinker who wants to get serious." It was British Royal Navy Surgeon General Sir Thomas Gimlette who introduced Rose's Lime Juice as a means of inducing sailors to take lime juice as anti-scurvy medication (it's why they were called "Limeys"). Gently-spiced rosemary syrup proves a more sophisticated companion to a crisp, full-bodied gin, and the dynamics are further enhanced by muddling the "good grass" of fresh rosemary to release aromatics of lemon and pine.

Ingredients:

1 sprig rosemary (plus 1 sprig for garnish)
1 1/2 ounces gin
1/2 ounce dry vermouth
1/2 ounce spiced rosemary syrup*
fresh-squeezed juice of 1/2 lime

Method:

Add 1 sprig of rosemary to a mixing glass and muddle gently while keeping the leaves intact. Fill the glass two-thirds full of ice cubes. Add the gin, vermouth, rosemary syrup, and lime juice. Shake vigorously and double strain into a pre-chilled cocktail glass. Garnish with sprig of rosemary.

*In a small saucepan over medium heat, combine 1 cup water, 3/4 cups turbinado sugar, 2 rosemary sprigs, 1 bay leaf, and 1/2 teaspoon black peppercorns. Bring to a boil, stirring, until sugar has dissolved. Remove from heat and allow to cool. Strain and refrigerate.

Yield: 1 drink

La Nueva Violeta
Josh Rademacher
Trinity and the Pope, Asbury Park, NJ

The rarity of Crème de Violette once appeared as a plot device in an episode of the 1960s British television series *The Avengers*, and in an earlier era it was an essential ingredient in both the Aviation and Mood Indigo cocktails. The evasive liqueur's blend of berries, vanilla, spices, and violet petals provides an understated sweetness to the preparation, energized with sparkling ginger beer (ginger ale with an extra ginger kick).

Ingredients:

1 1/2 ounces gin
1/2 ounce Crème de Violette
dash fresh-squeezed lemon juice
2 to 4 ounces ginger beer
dash lemon bitters
violet petals, for garnish

Method:

Combine the gin, Crème de Violette, and lemon juice with ice in a shaker. Shake vigorously and strain into a pre-chilled highball glass over fresh ice. Top with ginger beer and lemon bitters. Garnish with violet petals.

Yield: 1 drink

THE FROBISHER
JACKSON CANNON
EASTERN STANDARD, BOSTON, MA

Sir Martin Frobisher, the English seaman and explorer who sought a Northwest route to the spices of India and China, provides the *nom de guerre* for Mr. Cannon's spicy aperitif. With the Martinez cocktail (the great-grandfather of the Martini) as a frame of reference, the botanicals of gin are supplemented with alluring citrus, clove and vanilla aromatics from the vermouth, intermingling with cherry and almond notes from the maraschino liqueur. A squeeze of orange peel bathes the drink in a mist of precious oils.

Ingredients:

2 ounces gin
3/4 ounce Cinzano Rosé Vermouth
1/4 ounce Luxardo Maraschino Liqueur
strip of orange peel (white part removed)
maraschino cherry, for garnish

Method:

Combine the gin, vermouth, and cherry liqueur in a mixing glass filled with ice. Stir to chill and strain into a pre-chilled cocktail glass. Twist the orange peel over the surface, rub around rim of the glass, and discard. Garnish with the maraschino cherry.

Yield: 1 drink

HEATHER IN QUEUE
JACKSON CANNON
EASTERN STANDARD, BOSTON, MA

It was christened for a regular Friday-night patron who was standing "in queue" when Mr. Cannon created this drink as a replacement for her usual "Hoskins" (the bar ran out of Amer Picon). He remixed, retooled, and repurposed the familiar formula, combining a full-bodied gin with herbal-rich, cognac-based orange liqueur and a bitter, aromatic amaro for a satisfying complexity and lingering finish.

Ingredients:

1 1/2 ounces gin
3/4 ounce French vermouth
1/2 ounce Royal Combier Orange Liqueur
1/4 ounce Fernet Branca
lemon peel medallion

Method:

Combine the gin, vermouth, orange liqueur, and Fernet Branca in a mixing glass filled with ice. Stir to chill and strain into a pre-chilled cocktail glass. Squeeze lemon peel over surface to express oils and drop into the cocktail.

Yield: 1 drink

COCKTAIL VINO
KEENAN AHLO
BOKA KITCHEN + BAR, SEATTLE, WA

The tannins of red wine illuminate this elegant "witchcraft" with fruit notes from the wine upfront, rich botanicals of gin combined with the mint and fennel of Strega (the word for "witch" in Italian), and a hint of sweet citrus. Mr. Ahlo employs a Hawthorne strainer combined with an OXO fine mesh strainer to achieve a perfectly "smooth" cocktail surface, with no lemon pulp from the squeeze or ice chips from the shaking.

Ingredients:

1 3/4 ounces gin
1/4 ounce Liquore Strega
1/2 ounce fresh-squeezed lemon juice
1/2 ounce simple syrup
dry red wine

Method:

Combine the gin, Strega, lemon juice, and simple syrup with ice in a shaker. Shake vigorously and double strain into a pre-chilled cocktail glass. Pouring slowly over the back of a bar spoon, float just enough wine to cover the surface of the drink.

Yield: 1 drink

SGT. PEPPER
ERIKA FREY
CYRUS, HEALDSBURG, CA

In Napa Valley, Ms. Frey's cocktail offers perfect counterpoint to a day of wine tasting. Influenced by the progressive kitchen, she uses the *sous vide* ("under vacuum") technique to increase the strength of a pepper infusion. Since heat aids in the extraction of flavor, this method achieves results similar to a room-temperature infusion, but in less time and with a smaller amount of ingredients. The sealed environment minimizes effects on the gin, allowing vapor to re-condense into the liquid.

Ingredients:

1 1/2 ounces pepper-infused gin*
1/2 ounce fresh-squeezed lemon juice
1/2 ounce fresh-squeezed lime juice
1/2 ounce 2:1 simple syrup
Maldon Smoked Sea Salt, for garnish
mole foam, for garnish (optional)**

Method:

Fill a mixing glass one-half full of crushed ice. Add the gin, lemon juice, lime juice, and simple syrup. Shake lightly and pour into a highball glass with a smoked sea salt rim. Add a dollop of mole foam on top.

* Add 1 cup (8 ounces) gin, 1/2 Anaheim pepper, 1/2 jalapeno pepper, and 1/2 orange bell pepper into a vacuum-sealed zip-lock bag. Heat a pot of water to 140-degrees F., add the bag and cook *sous vide* for 20 minutes. Maintain even temperature by leaving a thermometer attached to the side of the pot.

** Whip 2 egg whites into a froth and mix with 1/2 ounce lemon juice, 1/2 ounce simple syrup, and 1/2 ounce mole spice rub. Chill and then charge in a whipped cream canister.

Yield: 1 drink

CORNUCOPIA
ERIKA FREY
CYRUS, HEALDSBURG, CA

The word verjus derives from the French term *vert jus*, literally the "green juice. It refers to wine grapes, picked from the vines just when the crop is beginning to ripen and pressed into juice. Savory organic vegetables and herbs from nearby Love Farms, their flavors heightened with the sweet-tart taste of verjus, provide the adventurous culinary landscape for a gin cocktail. This is, after all, wine country terrain.

Ingredients:

2 teaspoons fresh corn
small handful cilantro (reserve 1 leaf for garnish)
pinch of celery salt
1 1/2 ounces gin
1/2 ounce fresh-squeezed lemon juice
1/2 ounce 2:1 simple syrup
1/2 ounce Verjus Blanc
1/4 ounce Biotta Celery Juice
pickled baby corn, for garnish

Method:

In a mixing glass, muddle together corn and cilantro with the celery salt. Fill the mixing glass two-thirds full of ice cubes. Add the gin, lemon juice, simple syrup, verjus, and celery juice. Shake vigorously and double strain into a pre-chilled rocks (or lowball) glass. Garnish with pickled baby corn and cilantro leaf.

Yield: 1 drink

GIN-GIN
LEAH HOUGHTALING
FELICIA'S ATOMIC LOUNGE, ITHACA, NY

In the spirit of the Italian cin cin, Ms. Houghtaling's cocktail suggests celebration or commemoration. As the botanicals of gin mingle with sparkling wine, bubbles ripple to the top of the glass, breaking the surface in gentle bursts. When it's drawn to your lips, the aromatics reveal a fusion of vibrant components. With each sip, ginger, lemongrass, and maple notes warm and sweeten the palate. (Any brut type of sparkling wine is appropriate, not just Champagne. The drinksmith favors Spanish Cava.)

Ingredients:

1 1/4 ounces gin
3/4 ounce ginger-lemongrass syrup*
Brut Champagne or sparkling wine, to top up
candied ginger, for garnish

Method:

Combine the gin and ginger-lemongrass syrup in a mixing glass filled with ice. Stir to chill and strain into a pre-chilled Champagne flute. Slowly top up with Champagne. Garnish with a piece of candied ginger.

*Combine 1/4 cup fresh-grated ginger, 2 finely-chopped lemongrass stalks, 1 cup water, 1/4 cup maple sugar, and 1/4 cup sugar in medium saucepan over medium heat. Stir until sugar is dissolved. Simmer for 20 minutes (do not boil). Remove from heat and strain. Bottle and chill until ready to use.

Yield: 1 drink

RISING SUN
CHARLES JOLY
THE DRAWING ROOM, CHICAGO, IL

The ancient Japanese were unaware of any land east of their islands, and believed theirs was the first place on earth awakened by the rising sun. Characters that make up Japan's name mean "sun-origin," and the country is referred to as the "Land of the Rising Sun." Profoundly Japanese in imagery and ethos, Mr. Joly's veneration calls for an earthy-style gin to support the dazzling complexity of flavors.

Ingredients:

8 fresh basil leaves (plus 1 for garnish)
1/4 ounce yuzu juice
1/2 ounce fresh-squeezed grapefruit juice
3/4 ounce green tea-ginger syrup*
1/4 ounce fresh-squeezed lemon juice
1 1/2 ounces gin
lemon peel, cut into spiral, for garnish

Method:

Add basil, yuzu, grapefruit, green tea-ginger syrup, and lemon juice into a mixing glass. Muddle, gently, until the mixture is equal parts juice and solids. Add the gin and ice cubes. Shake vigorously and double strain into a pre-chilled coupe. Garnish with basil leaf wrapped in lemon spiral.

*Heat 16 ounces simple syrup until steaming. Add 4 premium green tea bags and 4 ounces of chopped ginger. Remove from heat, cover and let steep for 20 minutes. Strain and allow to cool. Refrigerate until ready to use.

Yield: 1 drink

FORBIDDEN FRUIT
CHARLES JOLY
THE DRAWING ROOM, CHICAGO, IL

A Windy City iconoclast, Mr. Joly delights in challenging established convention and tradition. And while clearing the palate with a crisp, gin-based cocktail before a meal is accepted custom, his consummation of gin with Grand Marnier (the quintessential digestif) and a "fruit cocktail" of flavors creates a liberating and satisfying after dinner drink.

Ingredients:

1/2 ounce Absinthe, for rinse
1 1/2 ounces gin
3/4 ounce Grand Marnier
3/4 ounce fresh pear puree
1/2 ounce fresh-squeezed lime juice
1/4 ounce fresh pineapple juice
lime peel, cut into spiral, for garnish
fresh pear slice, for garnish

Method:

Season a coupe with ice and Absinthe; swirl and dump. Combine the gin, Grand Marnier, pear puree, lime juice, and pineapple juice with ice in a shaker. Shake vigorously and strain into the coupe. Garnish with lime spiral and slice of pear.

Yield: 1 drink

CUCUMBER SMASH
SCOTT EVANS
PAGO, SALT LAKE CITY, UT

Cucumbers have long provided culinary ornament for the Pimm's Cup, an upper-crust tipple with gin, quinine, and a mixture of herbs, first served in a London oyster bar in 1823. In his seasonal cocktail rotation, Mr. Evans offers a summertime "smash," in which gin becomes a canvas for the fresh, subtle flavor of cucumber, its sensory profile further expanded with Hendrick's, a small-batch Scottish gin infused with a perfume-like essence of cucumber.

Ingredients:

3 slices cucumber (plus 1 slice for garnish)
5 sprigs cilantro (plus 1 sprig for garnish)
2 mint leaves
2 basil leaves
juice of 1/2 lime
1/2 ounce cilantro syrup*
1 1/2 ounces gin
club soda, to top up

Method:

Add cucumber, cilantro, mint, basil, lime juice, and cilantro syrup into a mixing glass. Muddle, gently, until the mixture is equal parts juice and solids. Add the gin and ice cubes. Shake vigorously and double strain into a pre-chilled rocks glass. Top up with the club soda. Garnish with cucumber slice and sprig of cilantro.

*In a small saucepan, combine 1/2 cup sugar, 1/4 cup water, and 2 sprigs of cilantro (stems and leaves) over medium heat, stirring occasionally until boiling. Continue to boil until the mixture is reduced by one-fourth. Bottle and chill until ready to use.

Yield: 1 drink

THE CLEAN GETAWAY

ANDY MINCHOW
HOLEMAN & FINCH PUBLIC HOUSE, ATLANTA, GA

Amaro means "bitter" in Italian, and the herbal, aromatic digestif is most often served neat, with a citrus wedge and a topping of tonic water to cleanse the palate after a big meal. Mr. Minchow employs gin as a convivial base for the time-honored bitter and citrus combination, while a sweet, sparkling cousin of Asti Spumante adds not only effervescence, but an air of festivity to this refreshing cocktail.

Ingredients:

1 ounce gin
1/2 ounce Amaro
1/2 ounce fresh lemon juice
2 ounces Moscato d'Asti

Method:

Build gin, Amaro, and lemon juice over ice in an Old Fashioned tumbler. Top with the sparkling wine. Stir gently.

Yield: 1 drink

WOLF'S BITE
ANDY MINCHOW
HOLEMAN & FINCH PUBLIC HOUSE, ATLANTA, GA

For his "ferocity and courage," Mr. Minchow's fellow Public House mixologist Greg Best is called "Wolf." The nickname, combined with a spicy, pungent "bite" of Chartreuse, suggests the moniker for a unique and assertive cocktail. To temper the botanical and herbal flavors and aromatics of gin and Chartreuse, the trick is the tart foil of citrusy grapefruit.

Ingredients:

1 1/2 ounces gin
1/2 ounce Chartreuse (green)
1 ounce fresh-squeezed grapefruit juice

Method:

Combine all ingredients with ice in a shaker. Shake vigorously and double strain into a pre-chilled martini glass. Serve without garnish.

Yield: 1 drink

EAST OF EDEN
JEFFREY MORGENTHALER
CLYDE COMMON, PORTLAND, OR

Its name inspired by Willamette Valley's East Valley wine trail, Mr. Morgenthaler employs a Gewurztraminer from Oregon wine country as an unexpected component in his stylish cocktail. Reduced to a syrup, the distinctive varietal adds a complexity of flavors and taut structure to the formula, lifting the lovely botanicals of gin, floral notes of elder-flower liqueur, and citrus fragrance of lemon.

Ingredients:

1 1/2 ounces gin
3/4 ounce fresh-squeezed lemon juice
1/2 ounce Gewurztraminer syrup*
1/4 ounce St. Germain Elderflower Liqueur
1/2 egg white
lemon peel medallion

Method:

Combine the gin, lemon juice, Gewurztraminer syrup, elderflower liqueur, and egg white with ice in a shaker. Shake vigorously and double strain into a pre-chilled cocktail glass. Squeeze lemon peel over surface to express oils and drop into the cocktail.

*In a medium saucepan over medium-high heat, reduce a 750-ml bottle of Gewurztraminer by half. Add 12 ounces of sugar to the hot liquid. Stir to thoroughly combine. Bottle and chill until ready for use.

Yield: 1 drink

BITTERSWEET SYMPHONY
JEFFREY MORGENTHALER
CLYDE COMMON, PORTLAND, OR

Like the conductor of a musical work, Mr. Morgenthaler directs a careful balance of power and grace, a swirl of contrasting notes in a captivating composition.   No baton, instead a long-handled bar spoon to stir a botanical-rich gin together with a blend of Punt e Mes ("point and a half"), a distinctive 15-herb vermouth with "point" of sweetness and "half a point" of bitterness, and Aperol, an aromatized aperitif whose formula includes bitter and sweet oranges and an infusion of herbs and roots.

Ingredients:

1 1/2 ounces gin
3/4 ounce Aperol
3/4 ounce Punt e Mes
lemon peel medallion

Method:

Combine the gin, Aperol, and Punt e Mes in a mixing glass filled with ice. Stir to chill and strain into a pre-chilled cocktail glass. Squeeze lemon peel over surface to express oils and drop into the cocktail.

Yield: 1 drink

THE FLAMINGO
DOMINIQUE GONZALES
ZOCALO, SACRAMENTO, CA

The Orange Blossom cocktail was introduced during Prohibition, an attempt to mask the taste of bathtub gin by drowning it in sweet orange juice. In an antithetical and more sophisticated formula, Ms. Gonzales lessens the measure of orange juice, allowing gin to hold center stage. Natural citrus sweetness is enhanced with agave, enough to temper the bitter notes of Campari without compromising its herbal complexity.

Ingredients:

1 1/2 ounces gin
3/4 ounce fresh-squeezed orange juice
1/2 ounce Campari
1/4 ounce agave nectar
dash Benedictine
dash orange bitters

Method:

Combine all ingredients with ice in a shaker. Shake vigorously and double strain into a pre-chilled coupe. Serve without garnish.

Yield: 1 drink

CUCUMBER MOJITONICO

ADAM SEGER
NACIONAL 27, CHICAGO, IL

Kingsley Amis, the British comic novelist, once observed that "hilarity and drink are connected in a profoundly human, peculiarly intimate way." He was not only a disciplined writer, but a serious drinker and among the first to recognize the affinity between spirits and the cucumber. Bar Chef Seger, who reserves a plot of fruits and vegetables at a local organic farm, marries the herbaceous flavors of gin with cucumber and a mix of herbs in a delightfully spry cocktail.

Ingredients:

Kosher salt, for garnish
fresh-cracked pepper, for garnish
5 slices cucumber (plus 1 for garnish)
1 lime, cut into eighths (white center pith removed)
1 handful of mixed herbs, i.e. basils, lemon thyme, tarragon, rosemary (reserve a few pieces for garnish)
2 ounces gin
tonic water, to top up

Method:

Rim a 16-ounce pint glass with the salt and pepper. Add cucumber, lime, and herbs. Muddle until juicy and aromatic. Add the gin, and stir gently. Fill with ice, and top up with the tonic. Garnish with a cucumber slice and herbs.

Yield: 1 drink

THE ITALIAN CUP
CLIF TRAVERS
BAR CELONA, BROOKLYN, NY

There is a sense that Mr. Travers is interlocking parts in a puzzle, as he seamlessly blends the lovely botanicals of gin with Cynar, the Italian bitter aperitif liqueur enriched from a fusion of herbs and plants, predominantly artichokes. Rather than clashing, the two ingredients play well together, a tot of fresh lime juice muting the harsher aspects of each.

Ingredients:

4 pieces cucumber, cut into 1-inch cubes (plus 1 spear for garnish)
3 Thai basil leaves (plus 1 leaf for garnish)
1 ounce simple syrup
3/4 ounce fresh-squeezed lime juice
1 ounce Cynar
1 1/2 ounces gin
tonic water, to top up

Method:

Add cucumber, basil, and simple syrup into a mixing glass. Muddle, gently, until the mixture is equal parts juice and solids. Add lime juice, Cynar, and gin. Fill two-thirds full of ice cubes. Shake vigorously and double strain into a tall glass filled with ice. Top up with the tonic. Garnish with cucumber spear and basil leaf.

Yield: 1 drink

TAX RELIEF
CLIF TRAVERS
BAR CELONA, BROOKLYN, NY

He has a penchant for refinement and explicit reference. Both tendencies unfold in Mr. Travers' fanciful update of the 1940s Income Tax Cocktail, a variation of the classic Martini with gin, sweet and dry vermouth, orange juice, and Angostura bitters. The drink originated at the old Waldorf Astoria Hotel bar with the Bronx Cocktail, then morphed into the Income Tax with the addition of bitters. (It could be said that paying one's income tax is a bitter experience).

Ingredients:

2 ounces gin
1/4 ounce Lillet Blanc
1/4 ounce Punt e Mes
1/4 ounce Rioja syrup*
2 dashes orange bitters
grapefruit peel medallion

Method:

Combine the gin, Lillet, Punt e Mas, Rioja syrup, and bitters with ice in a shaker. Shake vigorously and double strain into a pre-chilled cocktail glass. Squeeze grapefruit peel over surface to express oils and drop into the cocktail.

* In a medium saucepan over medium-high heat, reduce 1 cup of Rioja (red table wine) by half. Add 1/2 cup of sugar to the hot liquid. Stir to thoroughly combine. Bottle and chill until ready for use.

Yield: 1 drink

THE SECRET LIFE
PIP HANSON
CAFÉ MAUDE, MINNEAPOLIS, MN

Think of it as a refreshing intermezzo, cleansing the palate between courses of a festive dinner party, slowing down the dining experience to make a meal more enjoyable and meaningful. The presence of Champagne always represents an explosion of possibilities with gin.

Ingredients:

1 1/2 ounces gin
1 ounce honey syrup (blended honey 2:1 hot water)
1/2 ounce fresh-squeezed lemon juice
1 dash salt solution (3 parts hot water to 1 part kosher salt)
1/2 egg white
Champagne or sparkling wine, to top off
lemon wheel, for garnish

Method:

Combine the gin, honey syrup, lemon juice, salt solution, and egg white with ice in a shaker. Shake vigorously and strain into a pre-chilled Champagne flute (should fill about 2/3). Top up with Champagne. Garnish with a lemon wheel, placed across the rim of the flute.

Yield: 1 drink

DOUBLE DOUBLE
PIP HANSON
CAFÉ MAUDE, MINNEAPOLIS, MN

Ever the contrarian, Mr. Hanson rebels by turning to an old classic. And not just any old classic — it is with inspiration of the Negroni that he arrives at the elements of his composition. While the old master bartender at Caffè Casoni in Florence, Italy, strengthened the Americano cocktail with gin in 1919, Hanson's *formula moderna* elevates the aperitif with two vermouths and two herbal bitters.

Ingredients:

1 1/2 ounces gin
3/4 ounce Campari
1/2 ounce Carpano Antica Formula
1/2 ounce Carpano Punt E Mes
1/4 ounce Cynar
orange peel medallion

Method:

Combine the gin, Campari, Punt e Mas, Antica Formula, and Cynar in a mixing glass filled with ice. Stir to chill and strain into a pre-chilled rocks glass. Squeeze orange peel over surface to express oils and drop into the cocktail.

Yield: 1 drink

POMELO & BASIL SOUR
DEBBI PEEK
THE BRISTOL, CHICAGO, IL

In another era, the highball mix of gin and grapefruit juice was called a
Greyhound (served in a glass with a salted rim, it became a Salty Dog).
The gin-grapefruit partnership has been given new life as the base of a
balanced and sophisticated cocktail by Ms. Peek, with added citrus of
lime and licorice-scented basil. The cleverly constructed potation is
sipped through a contrasting and slightly-bitter layer of foam. It's like
a kiss that ends in a playful bite.

Ingredients:

1 ounce fresh-squeezed Pomelo or other pink grapefruit juice
1 ounce lime sour (equal parts fresh-squeezed lime juice and simple
syrup)
3 fresh basil leaves (plus 1 leaf for garnish)
1 1/2 ounces gin
3 dashes grapefruit bitters
Campari foam*

Method:

Add grapefruit juice, lime sour, and basil leaves into a mixing glass.
Muddle, gently, until the mixture is equal parts juice and solids. Add
gin and ice cubes. Shake vigorously and double strain into a pre-
chilled coupe. Top with Campari foam and bitters. Garnish with a
single basil leaf.

*Add 1/2 ounce lime sour, 1/2 ounce Campari, and 1 egg white into a
mixing glass and foam with a hand latte frother. Pour slowly over the
back of a bar spoon to float on top of the drink, taking care that it does
not mix with the other ingredients.

Yield: 1 drink

SOLANACEAE
DEBBI PEEK
THE BRISTOL, CHICAGO, IL

Embracing a philosophy one might call "farm to bar," Ms. Peek calls on fresh local produce to play as important a role as the spirit. A species of "Solanaceae" or nightshade plants, tomatoes lend their own natural balance between sweetness and acidity to a spirited blend with botanical-rich gin as a foil. Two shakes of the Worchester Sauce bottle put an exclamation point on this countrified preparation — with a nod to the savory kitchen.

Ingredients:

1/2 ounce fresh-squeezed lemon juice
1/2 ounce fresh-squeezed lime juice
1 ounce 2:1 simple syrup
6 heirloom cherry tomatoes, halved
6 fresh oregano leaves
1 sprig of fresh thyme
2 dashes Worchestershire Sauce
1 1/2 ounces gin

Method:

In an Old-Fashioned tumbler, muddle all ingredients except the gin. Add gin and ice. Stir gently.

Yield: 1 drink

BBC
ZAHRA BATES
PROVIDENCE, LOS ANGELES, CA

Her focused and nuanced approach to the cocktail is on display in Ms. Bates' sophisticated take on the reliable gin and cucumber combination. Aromas and flavors blend to create a thirst quencher that is bright, floral, and green, its ambiance reminiscent of a lush English garden. The anise flavor and fragrance of basil is unlocked by stacking leaves on top of one another, rolling into a cylinder, and cutting crosswise into fine shreds with a sharp knife — a technique called "chiffonade."

Ingredients:

3 medium basil leaves (+ 1 leaf for garnish)
2 ounces gin
3/4 ounce cucumber juice
1/2 ounce St. Germain Elderflower Liqueur
1/4 ounce fresh-squeezed lemon juice
dash bitters
Champagne, to top up

Method:

Chiffonade 3 basil leaves and drop into a mixing glass. Add the liquids (except Champagne) and ice cubes; shake vigorously. Pour into a Collins glass. Top up with the Champagne.

Yield: 1 drink

RINCON MARTINI
ZAHRA BATES
PROVIDENCE, LOS ANGELES, CA

She expands the boundaries of the cocktail with inspiration from the kitchen, and names a Martini for the chef who taught her the secret of roasting grapes. Ms. Bates employs the technique to concentrate the sugars and intensify the flavors, deftly building off gin's strong botanic backbone. The result is something that is at once sweet and savory, brilliantly accented with verjus (the juice of unripened grapes) and herbal liqueur.

Ingredients:

10 roasted green seedless grapes*
1 wedge honeydew melon (1/8 of 6 to 7-inch diameter), skin removed, cubed
2 ounces gin
1/4 ounce Verjus Blanc
1/4 ounce Biancosarti or Chartreuse (yellow)
honeydew melon slice, for garnish

Method:

Muddle grapes and melon in a mixing glass. Add the gin, verjus and liqueur. Stir to combine. Strain into a new mixing glass and discard the solids. Add ice cubes, shake vigorously, then fine-strain into a pre-chilled Martini glass.

*Preheat oven to 350-degrees F. Arrange grapes in a single layer on a baking sheet. Add a pinch of salt and roast (without oil) until the skins are slightly crisp but the grapes are still soft and juicy inside, about 15 minutes. Cool in fridge until ready to use.

Yield: 1 drink

FALL OF MAN
DAVID MOO
QUARTER BAR, BROOKLYN, NY

In the *Book of Genesis*, paradise is lost ts Adam and Eve after they sur-
render to the temptation of fruit from the forbidden tree, often symbol-
ized in art and literature as an apple tree. Inspired by the Prohibition-
era Bee's Knees cocktail (made with Applejack), Mr. Moo's latter-day
version includes fresh-pressed apple cider and sweet apple-flavored
liqueur. Blessed are the innovators.

Ingredients:

1 apple slice, 1/8-inch (plus 1 slice for garnish)
1/4 ounce Berentzen's Apfel Korn
1/8 ounce simple syrup
3/8 ounce fresh-pressed apple cider
1 dash orange bitters
2 1/2 ounces gin

Method:

Place apple slice into a mixing glass, and muddle to a pulp. Add
remaining ingredients, and fill two-thirds full of ice cubes. Shake
vigorously and double strain into a pre-chilled cocktail glass. Float
apple slice over the surface of the drink.

Yield: 1 drink

ALICE'S MALLET
DAVID MOO
QUARTER BAR, BROOKLYN, NY

There is a process for naming a cocktail, just as there is a method of its preparation. In this case, as Mr. Moo pondered a namesake for his gin-based formula, English gardens and garden parties came to mind. When someone suggested that the vivid, rhubarb-pink potion, perched on the "stilt" of a cocktail glass, looked remarkably like the flamingo used as a croquet mallet at *Alice in Wonderland's* mad garden party, the drink became "Alice's Mallet."

Ingredients:

1 ounce rhubarb syrup*
2 ounces gin
1 teaspoon orgeat syrup
1 teaspoon Aperol
1 teaspoon fresh-squeezed lemon juice
1 dash orange bitters

Method:

Combine all ingredients with ice in a shaker. Shake vigorously and strain into a pre-chilled coupe. Serve without garnish.

*Combine 2 cups of chopped rhubarb, 1/2 cup sugar, and 1/2 cup water in a heavy-bottomed sauce pan and bring to a boil. Lower the heat to a simmer and cook gently until the fruit is soft and the liquid has thickened slightly, about 20 minutes. Ladle into a fine strainer placed over a bowl. Strain to extract syrup. Cover and store in refrigerator until ready to use.

Yield: 1 drink

Ambassador
Jennifer Richtmyer
Grange Kitchen & Bar, Ann Arbor, MI

It was fictional secret agent James Bond who first partnered both gin and vodka in a Martini he called The Vesper, inspired by Vesper Lynd (a pun on "West Berlin") in 1953's *Casino Royale*. In the absence of the orange-flavor component, Kina Lillet, unavailable commercially since the 1960s, Ms. Richtmyer's homage to The Vesper includes orange-infused vodka, orange flower water, and the aromatics from a squeeze of the peel.

Ingredients:

1/2 teaspoon raw honey
1/2 ounce fresh-squeezed lemon juice
1 1/4 ounces gin
3/4 ounce Hangar One Mandarin Blossom vodka
2 drops Fee Brothers Orange Flower Water
orange peel medallion

Method:

In a mixing glass, muddle raw honey with lemon juice until smooth. Add the gin, vodka, and orange flower water, and fill two-thirds full of ice cubes. Shake vigorously and strain into a pre-chilled Martini glass. Squeeze orange peel over surface to express oils and drop into the cocktail.

Yield: 1 drink

TEA THYME

JENNIFER RICHTMYER
GRANGE KITCHEN & BAR, ANN ARBOR, MI

Taking tea is no longer bound by stuffy tradition, at least not in Ann Arbor. Ms. Richtmyer adds a satisfying kick of gin to tea made from the leaves and fruit of the black currant plant, a "shocking" departure from the domain of grannies and Ladies Who Lunch. The aroma is complex and multi-layered with lemony, slightly peppery notes of thyme, pungent, fruity aromas from the tea, coupled with the characteristic botanicals of the gin.

Ingredients:

1 1/4 ounces gin
3/4 ounce fresh-squeezed lemon juice
3/4 ounce thyme-infused simple syrup*
1 ounce strong-brewed black currant tea
lemon peel medallion

Method:

Combine the gin, lemon juice, simple syrup, and tea with ice in a shaker. Shake vigorously and strain into a pre-chilled Martini glass. Squeeze lemon peel over surface to express oils and drop into the cocktail.

*In medium saucepan over medium heat, stir together 3 ounces thyme, 1/2 cup water and 1/2 cup sugar until sugar dissolves. Slightly increase heat, simmer 5 minutes, stirring occasionally. Remove from heat and allow to cool down. Just before use, strain to remove the thyme.

Yield: 1 drink

GIN TIME AT THE "GONK"
RODNEY LANDERS
BLUE BAR, ALGONQUIN HOTEL, NEW YORK, NY

In 1910, a patron gave the Algonquin Hotel an antique grandfather clock to pay his outstanding bill. That clock became a meeting point at the "Gonk" for the Round Table, a group of New York City writers, actors, and wits, including Noel Coward who wrote, "For gin, in cruel sober truth, supplies the fuel for flaming youth." In Mr. Landers' liquid nod to hotel history, cucumber and thyme create a refreshing, earthy front, while the gin provides a long and gently warming finish.

Ingredients:

2 sprigs thyme (plus 1 sprig for garnish)
2 thin slices cucumber (plus 1 slice for garnish)
3/4 ounce fresh-squeezed lime juice
1/4 ounce 2:1 simple syrup
2 to 3 dashes orange bitters
2 ounces gin
3/4 ounce Cointreau

Method:

Add thyme, cucumber, lime juice, simple syrup, and orange bitters into a mixing glass. Muddle, gently, until the mixture is pulpy and fragrant. Add gin, Cointreau and ice cubes. Shake vigorously and double strain into a pre-chilled cocktail glass. Garnish with a sprig of thyme and slice of cucumber, placed across the lip of the glass.

Yield: 1 drink

THE STEADY COCKTAIL
DEREK BROWN
COLUMBIA ROOM, PASSENGER, WASHINGTON, DC

Equal parts gin and dry vermouth — this was the standard Martini formula in pre-Prohibition America. This deceptively simple cocktail is based on the old "Fifty-Fifty," yet while Mr. Brown retains historical proportion, he insists on using premium gin and a brand of very old, very good vermouth, uniting the botanicals of the gin and the aromatics of the vermouth with the herbaceous Elixir Végétal. "Stir over ice fifty times," implores the drinksmith, "the colder the better."

Ingredients:

1 1/2 ounces gin
1 1/2 ounces Dolin dry vermouth
3 drops Elixir Végétal de la Grande-Chartreuse

Method:

Combine all ingredients in a mixing glass filled with ice. Stir to chill and strain into a pre-chilled cocktail glass. Serve without garnish.

Yield: 1 drink

BLACK MISSION CUP
CLAIRE SPROUSE
BEAVER'S ICEHOUSE, HOUSTON, TX

She did not venture very far from home for inspiration. Native pear-shaped "Black Mission" figs, introduced to Texas by Spanish missionaries, thrive in the coastal areas outside Houston. Ms. Sprouse peels off the purplish-black skin, then purées the salmon-colored pulp to create a flavorful and textural component. The succulent fruit doesn't overpower; it adds delightful complexity to the locavore cocktail.

Ingredients:

5 ounces gin
1 ounce Pimm's No.1
3/4 ounce fresh-squeezed lemon juice
3/4 ounce 2:1 simple syrup
1 ounce Black Mission fig purée*
2 dashes Angostura bitters
club soda, to top up
mint sprig, for garnish
lemon wedge, for garnish

Method:

Combine gin, Pimm's, lemon juice, simple syrup, fig purée, and bitters with ice in a shaker. Shake vigorously and strain into an ice-filled Collins glass. Top up with club soda and garnish with mint sprig and lemon wedge.

*In a small saucepan, combine 2 cups fresh Black Mission figs, 1/2 cup water, and 2 ounces sugar over medium heat, stirring occasionally until boiling. Remove from heat, allow to cool, peel then purée the fruit until smooth. Cover and store in refrigerator.

Yield: 1 drink

VIOLET BEAUREGARDE
BRANDON CLEMENTS
SPRUCE, SAN FRANCISCO, CA

The drink is named for the fictional character in Roald Dahl's novel, *Charlie and the Chocolate Factory*, and like the precocious young lady, it is wonderfully complex, attractive to the eye, yet slightly bitter. Unlike Violet's unfortunate experience with magical chewing gum (she blows up into a giant blueberry), Mr. Clements' notion is a much less dramatic adventure with blueberries. It's an attractive work, painting gin in overtones of citrus and shades of blue.

Ingredients:

2 purple violets, for garnish
2 white violets, for garnish
5 fresh blueberries (plus 2 berries for garnish)
3/4 ounce lemongrass syrup*
3/4 ounce fresh-squeezed lemon juice
1 1/2 ounces gin
1/3 ounce Pagés Parfait Amour Liqueur
1 1/2 ounces Fever Tree Bitter Lemon
lemon peel spiral, for garnish
lavender sprig, for garnish

Method:

Fill a Collins glass with ice, interspersing violets throughout. Combine 5 blueberries, lemongrass syrup, and lemon juice in a mixing glass and muddle thoroughly. Add the gin and Parfait Amour, and fill with ice. Shake vigorously and double strain into the Collins glass. Top with the bitter lemon soda, and garnish with 2 blueberries, lemon peel spiral, and lavender sprig.

*Combine 1 cup sugar, 1 cup water, and 2 sliced lemongrass stalks (core only) in a small saucepan. Simmer over medium heat for 10 minutes, stirring to dissolve sugar. Remove from heat and cool. Strain into an airtight container and keep in refrigerator until ready to use.

Yield: 1 drink

THE DAIKON DREAM
CHRISTOPHER ROBERTS
PATOWMACK FARM, LOVETTSVILLE, VA

It started with an ingredient from the kitchen that begged for repurposing. "Mingling the aromatics of gin and the savory broth allow you to experience the drink before it is even sipped," explains Mr. Roberts. Just a splash of the more-vinegary-than-spicy fermented radish seems to coax out layers of botanicals in a deeply-flavored partnership that slowly grows on you. This is a show-stopping cocktail for any dinner party or Asian-inspired meal.

Ingredients:

3 1/2 ounces gin
1/4 ounce dongchimi broth*
2 one-inch discs of daikon radish (from marinade), for garnish
garlic scape, for garnish

Method:

Combine gin and dongchimi broth with ice in a shaker. Shake vigorously and strain into a pre-chilled Martini glass. Garnish with the radish discs and garlic scape.

*Peel and slice 8 medium Daikon radishes into 1-inch discs; peel and thinly slice 4 cloves of garlic; slice 4 green onions into 2-inch pieces. Coat the vegetables with 3 tablespoons of salt and 2 tablespoons of sugar. Let stand for one day at room temperature. After one day, dissolve 3 tablespoons of salt and 2 tablespoons of sugar into 1 quart of warm water. Add liquid to the salted vegetables, and let stand for two days at room temperature. When broth has achieved a tart, vinegary flavor, store in refrigerator until ready to use.

Yield: 1 drink

LION AND UNICORN
MIKE RYAN
SABLE KITCHEN AND BAR, CHICAGO, IL

The lion and the unicorn both appear on the royal coat of arms, the lion symbolizing England and the Unicorn a symbol for Scotland. In *Through the Looking Glass*, Lewis Carroll's subversive attack on England's imperialism, the lion and the unicorn are "fighting for the crown." In Mr. Ryan's warming cocktail, the "hostility" between gin and heat is tempered by the richness of sherry and comforting spices of chai. Lemon adds acidity for balance and clove adds sweet, spicy aromatics to the finish.

Ingredients:

1 1/2 ounce gin
1/2 ounce Lustau East India Sherry
1/2 ounce chai-infused demerara syrup*
1/2 ounce fresh-squeezed lemon juice
hot water, to top up
lemon peel spiral, studded with cloves, for garnish

Method:

Add the gin, sherry, demerara syrup, and lemon juice to a shaker, and heat in a water bath. Pour into a pre-heated toddy glass and top up with hot water. Garnish with clove-studded lemon peel.

*Combine 1 cup demerara sugar, 1/2 cup water, and 3 tablespoons chai spice blend in a saucepan over medium heat. Bring to a simmer, stirring until sugar and spices are dissolved. Remove from heat, let sit for one hour, then strain into an airtight container and keep in refrigerator until ready to use.

Yield: 1 drink

SARUMAN'S TOWER
MIKE RYAN
SABLE KITCHEN AND BAR, CHICAGO, IL

Rest your worn limbs and savor the frothy deliciousness that awaits your efforts. While *Lord of the Rings* may have inspired the name, an earlier drink, the 20th Century Cocktail (created to celebrate the Twentieth Century Limited train between New York City and Chicago), first suggested the partnership of gin and chocolate. Mr. Ryan's refreshment adds Cointreau for a burst of orange, egg white for creamy texture, and tonic water for a gently bitter finish.

Ingredients:

2 ounces gin
1/2 ounce Crème de Cacao (white)
1/2 ounce Cointreau
3/4 ounce fresh-squeezed lemon juice
1 egg white
tonic water, to top up
orange peel medallion

Method:

Combine the gin, Crème de Cacao, Cointreau, lemon juice, and egg white with ice in a shaker. Shake vigorously and strain into an ice-filled Collins glass. Top up with the tonic. Squeeze orange peel over surface to express oils and drop into the cocktail.

Yield: 1 drink

SOL REVIVER
SASHU MAGONDI & RAY CARRE
OM RESTAURANT & LOUNGE, CAMBRIDGE, MA

"Two levels of enlightenment" is how Solmon Chowdhury describes both his restaurant's ambiance and the sensory pleasure of his eponymous cocktail. Simultaneously bold and soothing, the gin and orange partnership draws inspiration from the vintage Orange Blossom cocktail, managing a graceful balance of botanicals and citrus. A rinse of Pernod adds a striking anise-flavored complexity to the restorative.

Ingredients:

1/4 ounce Pernod
2 ounces gin
3/4 ounce fresh-squeezed orange juice
3/4 Cointreau
2 dashes orange bitters
orange peel medallion

Method:

Rinse a pre-chilled cocktail glass with the Pernod. Discard excess. Combine the gin, orange juice, Cointreau, and bitters with ice in a shaker. Shake vigorously and strain into the cocktail glass. Squeeze orange peel over surface to express oils and drop into the cocktail.

Yield: 1 drink

FILL IN THE BLANC

DAN BAYHA
THE FOUNDRY ON MELROSE, LOS ANGELES, CA

The old saying "hair of the dog that bit you" is a common theory for curing a hangover, and the "hair of the dog" method — to simply keep drinking — has been around since alcohol was invented. In a kinder, gentler version of the old Hair of the Dog cocktail, Mr. Bayha keeps the gin, citrus element, and hot digestive aids to calm the stomach, but tempers the self-medication with a muddle of fresh cucumber.

Ingredients:

4 pieces cucumber, peeled, seeds removed, cut to 1/2-inch
1/2 ounce Lillet Blanc
1 dash Tabasco
1 pinch cayenne pepper
3 1/2 ounces gin
1 thin slice cucumber, for garnish
3 thin shreads of chile pepper, for garnish

Method:

Combine the cucumber sections, Lillet, Tabasco, and cayenne in a mixing glass and muddle thoroughly. Add the gin and fill with ice. Shake vigorously and double strain into a pre-chilled Martini glass. Garnish with cucumber slice and pepper shreads.

Yield: 1 drink

THE BATH HOUSE

DAN BAYHA
THE FOUNDRY ON MELROSE, LOS ANGELES, CA

While the communal bath house is an important part of traditional Japanese culture, the flavorful herb called "shiso" is an essential ingredient in traditional Japanese cuisine. Mr. Bayha decisively shapes the savor of a Far East-inspired cocktail with shiso's anise, citrus, and cinnamon overtones, a hint of cucumber, and a touch of pineapple sweetness. A quarter turn of the mill sends fresh-cracked pepper raining down, just enough to heighten aromatics.

Ingredients:

2 green shiso leaves
1 ounce cucumber water*
splash of pineapple juice
3 1/2 ounces gin
1 pinch fresh-cracked black peppercorns

Method:

Add the shiso leaves, cucumber water, and pineapple juice into a mixing glass. Muddle, gently, until the mixture is pulpy and fragrant. Add gin and ice cubes. Shake vigorously and double strain into a pre-chilled Martini glass. Grind a dusting of black pepper over the surface.

* Cut 1 cucumber into small chunks, place in a pint container and cover with water. Soak overnight in the refrigerator. Strain the mixture and discard the cukes.

Yield: 1 drink

GIN ESSENTIA
ELAD ZVI
BAR LAB, MIAMI, FL

His elegantly-crafted composition earns its preciousness with sweet licorice notes of thyme, smoky fragrance of cardamom, and a burst of fresh blackberry fruit. Tart citrus balances the sweetness of honey in Mr. Zvi's textural *chef-d'oeuvre*, while fresh sprigs of thyme coax out the plucky, herbal edge of juniper-forward gin.

Ingredients:

2 ounces gin
1 ounce herb-infused honey*
1 ounce blackberry syrup**
1 ounce fresh-squeezed lemon juice
2 drops Angostura bitters
2 sprigs thyme, for garnish

Method:

Combine gin, honey, blackberry syrup, lemon juice, and bitters with ice in a shaker. Shake vigorously and double strain into a pre-chilled cocktail glass. Garnish with sprigs of thyme.

*Combine 7 ounces of honey, 4 ounces of water, 4 sprigs of thyme, and 12 cardamom seeds in a small saucepan, and slowly bring to a boil. Remove from heat, let sit for one hour, then strain into an airtight container and chill in refrigerator.

** Lightly crush 10 ounces of fresh blackberries to release their juice. Strain juice into a small saucepan and simmer for 15 minutes. Add 3 drops of Angostura bitters and 2 drops of orange bitters. Remove from heat, let sit for one hour, then chill in refrigerator.

Yield: 1 drink

BUGIE (LIES)
MICHAEL SHEARIN
DRAGO CENTRO, LOS ANGELES, CA

Cocktails, like food, are about ingredients, and the "bar chef" takes his cue from the restaurant kitchen of Chef Celestino Drago. "Basil leaves make the drink more compatible with food," says Mr. Shearin, "while herbs and fresh lemon help to 'lift' the aromatic properties of the gin to create a sensuous palate complexity." Herbal and floral notes of the Dimmi Liquore meld seamlessly into the rich, soothing cocktail.

Ingredients:

6 fresh basil leaves (plus 1 leaf for garnish)
juice from 1/2 Meyer lemon
2 ounces gin
1 ounce Dimmi Liquore

Method:

Add 6 basil leaves and lemon juice into a mixing glass. Muddle, gently, until the mixture is pulpy and fragrant. Add gin, Dimmi Liquore and ice cubes. Shake vigorously and double strain into a pre-chilled Martini glass. Garnish with a single basil leaf.

Yield: 1 drink

Pozione Magica No. 2
Michael Shearin
Drago Centro, Los Angeles, CA

Even as we move ahead with all due speed, we must sometimes pause to honor the past. Mr. Shearin's "Magic Potion," his persuasive re-interpretation of the "exhumed" Corpse Reviver No. 2, is a case in point. Named for its purported ability to bring the dead (or at least painfully hungover) back to some semblance of life, the drink has been largely forgotten since the 1930s. Stirred into accord after an herbal rinse of Chartreuse and rhubarb/orange notes of Aperol, the revamped drink becomes a big, round, mouth-filling remedy.

Ingredients:

2 teaspoons Green Chartreuse, for rinse
1 ounce gin
1 ounce Aperol
1 ounce dry vermouth
1 ounce lemon juice
Maraschino cherry, for garnish

Method:

Pour the Green Chartreuse into a rocks glass and swirl to coat the glass; pour out any excess. Fill the glass with ice, add the gin, Aperol, dry vermouth, and lemon juice, and stir. Garnish with Maraschino cherry.

Yield: 1 drink

FAIRBANKS COCKTAIL
BILL DEGROOT
QUIESSENCE, PHOENIX, AZ

Rediscovery of the classics influences the development of vital, relevant cocktails. Mr. DeGroot can't explain how a variation of the Martini — one that replaced dry vermouth with Chartreuse — came to be called the Alaska Cocktail. But in his fling with the original formula, the cocktail takes the guise of a Gin Sour, adding lemon for the "sour" flavor, pineapple as sweetener, and egg white to build a snowy head.

Ingredients:

1 egg white
1/4 ounce fresh-squeezed lemon juice
2 ounces gin
3/4 ounce Chartreuse (yellow)
1 ounce Smalls Hand Foods Pineapple Gum Syrup
1 dash Bittercube Jamaican #1 Bitters
orange peel spiral "horseneck," for garnish*

Method:

Combine egg white and lemon juice in shaker tin, cover and shake vigorously for 1 minute to aerate the liquid. Add ice, gin, chartreuse, gum (gomme) syrup, and bitters to shaker; cover and shake vigorously for 1 minute. Strain into a chilled coupe. Garnish with orange horseneck.

*Carve a spiral peel continuously around the whole of an orange with a channel knife (makes about a 1/4 inch groove cut) to make one long strip, taking as little pith as possible.

Yield: 1 drink

THE PROVENÇALE
JASON KOSMAS & DUSHAN ZARIC
EMPLOYEES ONLY, NEW YORK, NY

Attired in kitchen whites, underscoring the culinary precision of their craft, "bar chefs" at Employees Only take a forward leap with the Martini construct, forsaking tradition and "purity" for an alluring cocktail with a view to the South of France. Lavender lends layers of floral and citrus, herbs de Provence add wondrous complexity, and orange richness of Cointreau provides the whiff of a captivating perfume.

Ingredients:

1 3/4 ounces lavender-infused gin*
1 1/4 ounces herbs de Provence-infused dry vermouth**
3/4 ounce Cointreau
orange peel medallion

Method:

Combine the gin, vermouth, and Cointreau in a mixing glass filled with ice. Stir to chill and strain into a pre-chilled cocktail glass. Squeeze orange peel over surface to express oils and drop into the cocktail.

* Add 1 1/2 teaspoons dried lavender to a 750-ml bottle of gin. Infuse for 24 hours, then strain and rebottle.

**Combine 2 1/4 teaspoons of herbes de Provence and 3/4 cup of dry vermouth (from a full 750-ml bottle) in a small saucepan over low-medium heat, and slowly bring to a simmer (not a boil). Simmer for 5 minutes, remove from heat and let cool. Strain infusion back into the bottle with the remainder of the vermouth.

Yield: 1 drink

ROSELLE
ROB KRUEGER
EMPLOYEES ONLY, NEW YORK, NY

The history of hibiscus as refreshment reaches back to the Pharaohs of the ancient Nile Valley who fortified themselves with infusions of flower petals against the desert heat. Rosella, botanical cousin of the more flamboyant ornamental hibiscus, provides Mr. Krueger an appealing tangy/sweet compliment to the botanicals of gin, the citrus richness of lime and grapefruit, and a jewel-like ruby coloring to the drink.

Ingredients:

1 1/2 ounces gin
1 ounce rosella (hibiscus) cordial*
3/4 ounce fresh-squeezed lime juice
1/2 ounce fresh-squeezed grapefruit juice

Method:

Combine all ingredients with ice in a shaker. Shake vigorously and strain into a pre-chilled cocktail glass. Serve without garnish.

*Remove the green seedpods from the calyxes of 6 to 8 rosellas. Place intact rosellas in a small saucepan and cover with water. Over medium-high heat, simmer until soft (and the red color has faded from the calyx). Remove from heat, and let steep for two hours. Strain the mixture (press down on the plant material to extract all liquid). Discard fruit and seeds. For every cup of liquid add a cup of sugar. Heat gently until all sugar is dissolved, stirring continually. Cover and store in refrigerator.

Yield: 1 drink

GINBOREE
RYAN GOLDEN
PLAN B BAR + KITCHEN, CHICAGO, IL

It's not hard to understand what enticed Mr. Golden to this formula. Finding the right balance in a mixed drink is a challenge that seasoned bartenders are ready, if not eager, to face. In his teasingly subtle and nuanced composition, basil, lemon, and cucumber serve as a culinary canvas for the botanical notes of gin, and preparation allows for a mid-course correction to assure sweet/sour equilibrium.

Ingredients:

small handful of basil
1/4 cucumber, quartered
half a lemon, quartered
1/2 (to 2/3) ounce 2:1 simple syrup
2 ounces gin
lemon peel medallion
1 slice cucumber, for garnish

Method:

Add the basil, cucumber, and lemon into a mixing glass. Muddle, gently, until the mixture is pulpy and fragrant. (Test the mix and, if desired, add additional simple syrup to adjust the sweet/sour balance). Add gin and ice cubes. Shake vigorously and double strain into a rocks glass filled with ice. Squeeze lemon peel over surface to express oils and drop into the cocktail. Garnish with cucumber slice.

Yield: 1 drink

GIN & GRIN
VICTORIA D'AMATO-MORAN
CENT'ANNI COCKTAILS, SAN FRANCISCO, CA

The cavalcade of ingredients speaks to the scope of her ambition, not to mention imagination. Ms. D'Amato-Moran's flavor combinations are earthy, savory, bright, and fresh in a luscious, palate-refreshing, pre-dinner "amuse." The composed cocktail is joyfully perfumed in Absinthe and served with playful garnishes that leave you grinning from ear to ear.

Ingredients:

1/2 celery stalk, sliced
1 pinch arugula
4 basil leaves
1 ounce fennel syrup*
1 1/2 ounces gin
1/2 ounce lime juice
3 ounces fresh cucumber juice
spritz Absinthe, for aromatics
cucumber ribbon, for garnish
celery leaf, for garnish
fennel fronds, for garnish

Method:

Add celery, arugula, basil, and fennel syrup into a mixing glass. Muddle, gently, until the mixture is pulpy and fragrant. Add gin, lime juice, cucumber juice, and ice cubes. Shake vigorously and strain into a Collins glass filled with ice. Spritz Absinthe over top from an atomizer. Garnish with cucumber ribbon, celery leaf, and fennel fronds.

*Thinly slice one fennel bulb and add to a sauce pan. Add 1 cup water and 1 cup sugar. Bring to a boil, then reduce heat and simmer for 10 minutes (syrup will thicken upon cooling).

Yield: 1 drink

PEAR SOIRÉE
VICTORIA D'AMATO-MORAN
CENT'ANNI COCKTAILS, SAN FRANCISCO, CA

It may be a stretch to call Ms. D'Amato-Moran a contemporary artist, but never mind. Her ability to make ingenious use of culinary ingredients is revelatory and relevant. "This recipe represents my passion for bringing the kitchen into my cocktails," explains Ms. D'Amato-Moran, who offers a dinner party recommendation: "My Pear Soirée is divine alongside a crispy Butter Leaf and Romaine Salad with Gorgonzola cheese and cayenne-spiced pecans."

Ingredients:

1 1/2 ounces gin
1 ounce lemon-spice syrup*
3 ounces Santa Cruz Organic Pear Nectar
lemon wheel, thinly-sliced, for garnish

Method:

Combine gin, lemon-spice syrup, and pear juice with ice in a shaker. Shake vigorously and strain over fresh ice in a double rocks glass. Float the lemon wheel on the surface of the drink.

* Add 1 1/2 cups lemon juice, 1/2 cup water, 2 cups sugar, 1 level teaspoon cinnamon, 1 whole nutmeg (ground), and 2 star anise to a saucepan. Bring to a boil, then reduce heat and simmer for 10 minutes. Cover and store in refrigerator.

Yield: 1 drink

ROCK 'N THYME
MARK STODDARD
THE BITTER BAR, BOULDER, CO

Provence is a captivating region, considered to be the garden of France and distinguished by its culinary character. Inspired by ingredients that loom large in Provençal cooking, Mr. Stoddard conjures a savory, soul-satisfying cocktail that is at once rustic and urban. His union of gin with sweet/sour and bittersweet components is an achievement and the ambrosial baked-apple aroma is a revelation.

Ingredients:

1 1/2 ounces gin
1 ounce thyme-lime syrup*
1/2 ounce Cynar Artichoke
3 dashes Bar Keep Organic Baked Apple Bitters
1 thin slice of apple, for garnish
1 sprig thyme, for garnish

Method:

Combine gin, thyme-lime syrup, Cynar, and apple bitters with ice in a shaker. Shake vigorously and double strain into a pre-chilled coupe. Garnish with apple slice and sprig of thyme.

*In a medium saucepan, combine 1 1/2 cups of water and 1 cup + 2 tablespoons of sugar. Bring to a boil, stirring to dissolve the sugar. Add 3/4 ounce of thyme sprigs, cover and let stand overnight. Add 3/4 cup of fresh-squeezed lime juice, strain into an airtight jar, and store in refrigerator.

Yield: 1 drink

TIROLO
LUKE McKINLEY
RAVISH, SEATTLE, WA

Aromatic Amaro is produced in the Lombardy region, bordering the Italian Alps, and suggesting a theme for Mr. McKinley's cocktail. "The herbal liqueur lures one in for the first sip," he explains, "while never overshadowing a flavorful, slightly-sweetened, Old Tom-style gin." His achievement is lovely to drink on the rocks, especially after dinner, as the tongue becomes accustomed to the citrus notes of Cointreau and restrained bitter finish.

Ingredients:

1 1/2 ounces gin
1/3 ounce Amaro Ramazzotti
1/2 ounce Cointreau
dash Angostura bitters

Method:

Combine all ingredients with ice in a shaker. Shake vigorously and strain over fresh ice into a rocks glass. Serve without garnish.

Yield: 1 drink

LIONS IN LONDON
GREGORY SEIDER
THE SUMMIT BAR, NEW YORK, NY

Not the least of Mr. Seider's talent is his inventiveness in contriving backdrop for an infused gin. His cocktail's appellation is a nod to the spirit's British roots, but its enhanced flavors and distinctive color originate from the "red bush" of South Africa. The sweet, slightly nutty influence of Rooibos tea leaves proves hospitable companion to both Aperol's herbal complexity and dried fruit character of the vermouth.

Ingredients:

2 ounces Roobios tea-infused gin*
3/4 ounce Aperol
1/2 ounce Dolin Rouge vermouth
2 dash orange bitters
orange peel medallion

Method:

Combine the infused gin, Aperol, and vermouth in a mixing glass filled with ice. Stir to chill and strain over fresh ice into a rocks glass. Squeeze orange peel over surface to express oils and drop into the cocktail.

* Add 3 tablespoons Roobios tea to 750-ml bottle of gin. Infuse for 24 hours, then strain and rebottle.

Yield: 1 drink

GIN BLOSSOM
JULIE REINER
CLOVER CLUB, BROOKLYN, NY

"The martini evolves," explains cocktail historian David Wondrich. "It has evolved since it was born." In this weightier rendition of the classic formula, developed by Ms. Reiner as the Clover Club's house Martini, Eau de Vie adds depth and complexity to the marriage of gin and vermouth, stirred over ice — never shaken — to achieve silky-smooth texture and crystal-clearness. (Gin blossom, by the way, is slang for the capillaries in your nose and face that burst due to excessive drinking).

Ingredients:

1 1/2 ounces gin
3/4 ounce Martini Bianco Vermouth
3/4 ounce Blume Marillen Apricot Eau de Vie
2 dashes orange bitters
orange peel medallion

Method:

Combine the gin, vermouth, Eau de Vie, and bitters in a mixing glass filled with ice. Stir to chill and strain into a pre-chilled Martini glass. Squeeze orange peel over surface to express oils and drop into the cocktail.

Yield: 1 drink

BASILLICO FRESCO
MUZLINA CASEY
CURE BAR AND BISTRO, WASHINGTON, DC

"My approach to creating cocktails is focused on maintaining the integrity of the primary ingredient," explains Ms. Casey. "In this drink, added flavors are intended as accessories to the predominant gin." Agave and lemon provide sweet/tart contrast; basil releases notes of licorice and clove; tonic water adds crisp sparkle. Ornamental, perfumed foam lends a dash of sophistication.

Ingredients:

5 sweet basil leaves (plus 1 leaf for garnish)
1/2 ounce agave nectar
1 ounce fresh-squeezed lemon juice
1 1/4 ounces gin
3 ounces tonic water
1 tablespoon cucumber-basil foam*

Method:

Add basil, agave, and lemon juice into a mixing glass. Muddle, gently, until the mixture is pulpy and fragrant. Add gin and ice cubes. Shake vigorously and strain into a Collins glass filled with ice. Add the tonic water and top with a generous tablespoon of the cucumber-basil foam. Garnish with basil leaf.

*Bloom 1/8 ounce of gelatin (about 2 sheets) in 1 ounce of cool water. Add 3 ounces of warm water and whisk in 10 ounces of cucumber juice (extract from juicer) and 2 ounces of fresh sweet basil puree. Chill and then charge in a whipped cream dispenser.

Yield: 1 drink

HERR NAPHTA

DAVID WHITTON AND SONNY BONASERA
VILLAINS TAVERN, LOS ANGELES, CA

The term for a mix of volatile liquids suggested the name for "Naphta," the revolutionist character in Thomas Mann's 1924 German novel, *The Magic Mountain (Der Zauberberg)*, as well as the name for a makeover of the nearly-forgotten Frisco cocktail. Its original rye whiskey component is replaced with a bracing blast of gin, while the syrupy sweetness of Benedictine is kept in check with a squeeze of tart, fresh-squeezed lemon.

Ingredients:

2 ounces gin
2/3 ounce Benedictine
2 dashes Bar Keep Swedish Herb Bitters
1/2 ounce fresh-squeezed lemon
orange peel medallion

Method:

Combine the gin, Benedictine, lemon juice, and bitters in an Old Fashioned tumbler. Add ice (preferably one large chipped cube) and stir. Squeeze orange peel over surface to express oils and drop into the cocktail.

Yield: 1 drink

JEAN BAPTISTE
JAMES GOAD
SLOW CLUB, SAN FRANCISCO, CA

The devil of Mr. Goad's drink is in the details. For example, he infuses a light, mild-flavored honey, allowing the savory, forward notes of sage to emerge. And for the herbal component, his choice of yellow rather than green Chartreuse assures a slightly sweeter, more aromatic companion to the gin. Flavors join together for a delicate waltz of sweet, floral, herbal and earthy tones.

Ingredients:

1 1/2 ounces gin
1/2 ounce Chartreuse (yellow)
3/4 ounce fresh-squeezed lime juice
1/2 ounce sage-infused honey*
3 dashes orange bitters
1 sage leaf, for garnish

Method:

Combine gin, Chartreuse, lime juice, infused honey, and orange bitters with ice in a shaker. Shake vigorously and strain into a pre-chilled coupe. Garnish with the sage leaf.

*Remove the lid from a 12 to 16-ounce jar of honey, and place the open jar in a small sauce pan with 2 inches of water. Gently heat the water until the honey is warm and runny. Carefully remove the jar and place 1/4 cup of chopped fresh sage at the top. Replace the lid and shake. Allow herbs to steep in a cool, dark place at least five days for maximum intensity. Reheat the jar to re-liquify the honey, then strain out the herbs.

Yield: 1 drink

MONARCH
JAMES GOAD
SLOW CLUB, SAN FRANCISCO, CA

Its name inspired by a grand old dame hotel on San Francisco's Nob Hill, Mr. Goad's cocktail steps up the botanically-intensive flavors of gin with Lillet Blanc, the lovely "eau de cologne" of white Bordeaux wines and citrus liqueurs. As if in response to the notes of bitter orange and grapefruit, the concoction is bathed in fresh fruit juices, while its sweetener is scented with the warm spices of Peychaud's.

Ingredients:

1 sugar cube (or 1 teaspoon granulated sugar)
3 or 4 shakes Peychaud's bitters
1 1/4 ounces gin
1/2 ounce Lillet Blanc
3/4 ounce fresh-squeezed lemon juice
1/2 ounce fresh-squeezed ruby red grapefruit juice
1/2 teaspoon grated orange zest, for garnish

Method:

In a mixing glass, douse the sugar cube with bitters and muddle to a slurry-like consistency. Add gin, Lillet, lemon juice, grapefruit juice, and ice cubes. Shake vigorously and strain into a Collins glass filled with ice. Garnish by zesting orange on top with a microplane.

Yield: 1 drink

COOL HAND LUKE
RYAN ANDREWS
LIEGE, OAKLAND, CA

Combining vodka and gin in a single cocktail, then taming the spirits with citrus and cucumber, dates all the way back to the World War I-era Vladivostok Virgin, a drink that Charles H. Baker Jr. once called "a risky little heart-warmer from out frozen Siberia." So Mr. Andrews' cocktail is less a discovery than a remarkable refinement, energizing the vodka-gin comradeship with bright, appealing flavors and penetrating, sweetly-floral aromatics.

Ingredients:

1-inch piece cucumber, cut into cubes (+3 thin slices for garnish)
1/2 ounce lavender syrup*
1/2 ounce fresh-squeezed lime juice
1 1/2 ounces vodka
1 ounce gin

Method:

Add cucumber cubes, lavender syrup, and lime juice into a mixing glass. Muddle, gently, until the mixture is pulpy and fragrant. Add vodka, gin and ice cubes. Shake vigorously and double strain into a pre-chilled coupe. Garnish with the cucumber slices.

*Combine 3/4 cup water, 1/2 cup turbinado or unrefined sugar, 2 fresh lavender blossoms (or 1 teaspoon dried) and 1 fresh basil leaf in a saucepan, and bring to a boil. Remove from heat, cover and let cool. Strain and refrigerate.

Yield: 1 drink

THE BOHANON
MAX TOSTE
DEEP ELLUM, ALLSTON, MA

His formula is by no means timid. Mr. Toste appropriates a punch bowl-inspired ingredient that harkens back to the 19th century and pre-Prohibition potions of "Professor" Jerry Thomas. He combines the insistent flavors of Swedish Punsch (Batavia Arrack combined with lemon peel, tea, vanilla, cardamom and nutmeg) and robustly herbal Chartreuse for an encounter with the botanicals of gin. A twist of the pepper mill adds a bit of heat to the sizzling finale.

Ingredients:

2 ounces gin
1/2 ounce Chartreuse (green)
1/2 ounce Batavia-Arrack van Oosten Swedish Punsch
1 dash orange bitters
fresh-ground black pepper, for garnish

Method:

Combine the gin, Chartreuse, Swedish Punsch, and bitters in a mixing glass filled with ice. Stir to chill and strain into a pre-chilled coupe. Grind a dusting of black pepper over the surface of the drink.

Yield: 1 drink

SMITTEN
BOBBY HEUGEL
ANVIL BAR & REFUGE, HOUSTON, TX

Describing the original Negroni cocktail, Orson Welles explained, "The bitters are excellent for your liver, the gin is bad for you — they balance each other." While Mr. Heugel's pre-dinner tipple includes equal parts Campari bitters and gin, his addition of citrus and sweetener blunts the intense bitterness of the classic, while fresh mint neither steals the show nor fades into the background.

Ingredients:

8 fresh mint leaves (plus 1 leaf for garnish)
1 ounce fresh-squeezed lemon juice
1/2 ounce simple syrup
1 ounce gin
1 ounce Campari

Method:

Add 8 mint leaves, lemon juice, and simple syrup into a mixing glass. Muddle, gently, until the mixture is pulpy and fragrant. Add gin, Campari and ice cubes. Shake vigorously and double strain into a pre-chilled cocktail glass. Float a mint leaf over the drink.

Yield: 1 drink

ORANGE BLOSSOM GIN

ROSS KUPITZ
DAMICO KITCHEN, MINNEAPOLIS, MN

"I like to ask people to taste this cocktail on its own," says Mr. Kupitz, "then have them lick a bit of the pistachio dust and taste it again." He explains that olive oil and toasted pistachios have a "flavor-tripping" effect that changes the taste of the drink, alerting the senses to the interplay of gin with floral, fruit, and herbal flavors without compromising the delicate balancing act. And texture — how the drink feels in the mouth — provides authority.

Ingredients:

olive oil
toasted pistachio dust**
2 fresh basil leaves (plus 1 leaf for garnish)
2 ounces gin
3/4 ounce St. Germain Elderflower Liqueur
3/4 ounce strawberry-orange blossom consommé*

Method:

Lightly brush the outside rim (about 1/4-inch) of a Collins glass with olive oil, and roll in the toasted pistachio dust. Tear and slap 2 basil leaves (do not muddle) to extract essential oils and place in a mixing glass. Add the gin, elderflower liqueur, fruit consommé, and ice. Shake vigorously and pour into the prepared glass without disturbing the dusted rim. Garnish with a single basil leaf.

*Cut 1/2 pint of fresh strawberries into slices and place in a small saucepan with 1/2 cup sugar, 1 cup orange blossom water, and 1/2 teaspoon each of lemon and orange zest. Bring to a boil, reduce heat, and simmer for 3 minutes. Strain and refrigerate.

** Toast 2 tablespoons of shelled pistachios in a 350-degree toaster for 5 to 6 minutes or until fragrant. Remove from toaster, allow to cool, and grind into a powder in a blender.

Yield: 1 drink

MAJOR PATRICK'S CUP

JOSÉ ANDRÉS
ZAYTINYA, WASHINGTON, DC

During World War II, Major Patrick Leigh Fermor played a prominent role behind the lines in the Battle of Crete. Disguised as a shepherd, he led a British team that captured the German Commander, ending Nazi occupation of the Greek island. Major Patrick, regarded as a Greek national hero, is saluted with a rejuvenated, more culinary version of the thirst-quenching British potation to accompany the Greek mezze menu of star chef José Andrés.

Ingredients:

cucumber, 2-inch piece, diced
2 sprigs fresh dill (plus 1 sprig for garnish)
1/2 ounce fresh-squeezed orange juice
2 dashes orange bitters
1 ounce gin
3 ounces Pimm's No. 1
1 1/2 ounces ginger ale
cucumber, sliced into ribbon, for garnish
1/2 teaspoon grated orange zest, for garnish

Method:

Add diced cucumber, dill, orange juice, and bitters into a mixing glass. Muddle quickly. Add gin, Pimm's, and ice cubes. Shake vigorously and double strain into a highball glass filled with ice. Add a splash of ginger ale. Garnish the ribbon of cucumber (artfully swirled in the glass), sprig of dill, and orange zest.

Yield: 1 drink

SAFFRON MOON IN A VIOLET SKY
ANDREW SHAPIRO
DINO, WASHINGTON, DC

At first you wonder why it seems so familiar. Indeed, a similar formula dates to 1940, devised by Oscar Tschirky, better known as "Oscar of the Waldorf," at the bar of the venerable New York City hotel. His recipe for the geriatric Blue Moon cocktail appeared on the back label of the Crème Yvette bottle, a berry-infused, violet-colored liqueur he paired with gin. With Mr. Shapiro's addition of dry vermouth, the drink makes a leap into prime Martini territory.

Ingredients:

1 1/2 ounces gin
3/4 ounce Dolin Blanc Vermouth
1/3 ounce Crème Yvette
3 dashes Fee Brothers Peach Bitters
lemon peel medallion

Method:

Fill a mixing glass two-thirds full of ice cubes. Add the gin, vermouth, Crème Yvette, and bitters. Stir to chill and strain into a pre-chilled coupe. Squeeze lemon peel over surface to express oils and drop into the cocktail.

Yield: 1 drink

GINGER SIDECAR
DARRYL ROBINSON
HUDSON BAR, NEW YORK, NY

The brandy-based Sidecar was created at the Hotel Ritz in Paris during World War I, and when gin replaced brandy, the cocktail became a Chelsea or London Sidecar. "Dr. Mixologist" Robinson advances the notion by introducing the savory influence of ginger with contrasting influences of lemon and pineapple juice. He varies ratios for just the right balance of sweet and sour, keeping faithful to the original sugar rim garnish.

Ingredients:

superfine sugar, for garnish
3 slices fresh ginger
1/2 ounce fresh lemon juice (+lemon peel to moisten glass)
1/2 ounce 2:1 simple syrup
1/2 ounce pineapple juice
1 ounce Canton Ginger Liqueur
2 ounces gin

Method:

Moisten the rim of a chilled Martini glass with a lemon peel and dip into superfine sugar to coat. Place ginger into a mixing glass, and muddle to a pulp. Add remaining ingredients, and fill two-thirds full of ice cubes. Shake vigorously and double strain into the prepared Martini glass.

Yield: 1 drink

Elixer G
Darryl Robinson
Hudson Bar, New York, NY

Palate complexity provides the dramatic device in his articulate composition. "Doctor Mixologist" Robinson moves beyond the traditional drink into a more adventurous culinary landscape, and while elderflower liqueur, cilantro leaves, raspberries, and a mix of citrus juices play supporting roles, he takes care to insure that gin remains the protagonist.

Ingredients:

8 fresh raspberries
6 fresh cilantro leaves (+ 1 leaf for garnish)
1/4 ounce fresh-squeezed lemon juice
1/4 ounce fresh-squeezed lime juice
1/4 ounce agave nectar
1/2 ounce elderflower liqueur
2 ounces gin

Method:

Add raspberries, 6 cilantro leaves, lemon juice, lime juice, and agave syrup into a mixing glass. Muddle, gently, until the mixture is pulpy and fragrant. Add elderflower liqueur, gin and ice cubes. Shake vigorously and double strain into a pre-chilled cocktail glass. Garnish with a single cilantro leaf.

Yield: 1 drink

THE DIPLOMAT
CHRISTOPHER FRANKEL
ANVIL BAR & REFUGE, HOUSTON, TX

Once nicknamed "ouvre l'appetit" ("open the appetite"), Gentiane-Quina is a French aperitif wine whose bitter gentian root and cinchona bark flavorings engage the bright botanicals of gin in Mr. Frankel's courtly stimulant. Add background notes of orange, cherry, almond and now, my friend, you've got yourself a drink.

Ingredients:

1 ounce gin
1 ounce Bonal Gentiane-Quina
1/2 ounce Combier Orange Liqueur
1 teaspoon Luxardo Maraschino Liqueur
1 dash orange bitters
orange peel medallion

Method:

Combine the gin, Gentiane-Quina, orange liqueur, Maraschino, and bitters in a mixing glass filled with ice. Stir to chill and strain into a pre-chilled cocktail glass. Squeeze orange peel over surface to express oils and drop into the cocktail.

Yield: 1 drink

GIN & SUN
AIMEE BERTANI
THE GILT CLUB, PORTLAND OR

It might seem a bit odd to infuse another flavor into gin, since gin is already abundantly flavored, but Ms. Bertani sets out to foil expectations with an ingredient more typically found in salad fixings. She macerates cucumbers in gin for three days, squeezes out every ounce of liquid, then adds bright, tart lime and a few shakes of celery bitters, all against a backdrop of mint. The result is a blissful, refreshing summertime sipper.

Ingredients:

8 fresh mint leaves (+1 mint leaf for garnish)
1 ounce fresh-squeezed lime juice
3 shakes celery bitters
2 ounces cucumber-infused gin*

Method:

Add 8 mint leaves, lime juice, and bitters into a mixing glass. Muddle, gently, until the mixture is pulpy and fragrant. Add infused gin and ice cubes. Shake vigorously and double strain into a Collins glass filled with ice. Float a mint leaf over the drink.

*Peel, seed, and dice 3 cucumbers. Place in a large pitcher or other container with a lid. Add the contents of a 750-ml bottle of gin and stir. Refrigerate for 3 days, stirring once per day. Strain the infusion through a fine mesh strainer into a measuring cup, removing as much liquid as possible from the cucumbers. Rebottle.

Yield: 1 drink

THE VERMONT COCKTAIL
PAUL MCGEE
THE WHISTLER, CHICAGO, IL

Attired in black vest and bow tie, the maestro reverently crafts a seasonal cocktail in which gin collides with Vermont maple syrup, apple and apricot brandies with just a hint of tart lime. Think of it as spiked fruit crisp in a glass, with familiar autumn flavors that seem to have a comforting sweetness and a natural affinity for each other.

Ingredients:

1 ounce gin
2 ounces Laird's Bonded Apple Brandy
1/4 ounce Marie Brizard Apry (apricot brandy)
3/4 ounce fresh-squeezed lime juice
1/2 ounce maple syrup (grade A)
3 dashes Angostura bitters

Method:

Combine all ingredients with ice in a shaker. Shake vigorously and double strain into a pre-chilled Old Fashioned tumbler. Serve without garnish.

Yield: 1 drink

MAROON ON BLACK
RYAN LOTZ
LINEAGE, BROOKLINE, MA

The name borrows from one of abstract expressionist Mark Rothko's murals, originally created for New York's Four Seasons restaurant, and often referred to as "background" art. In his liquid homage, Mr. Lotz unleashes brash flavors, much as the painter attacked his canvases with color. Caramel hues of bitter amaro mix with the yellow/gold essence of elderflower blossoms to create a soft-edge background for the gin.

Ingredients:

2 ounces gin
3/4 ounce St. Germain Elderflower Liqueur
3/4 ounce Amaro Ramazzotti
orange peel spiral "horseneck," for garnish*

Method:

Combine the gin, St. Germain, and Amaro Ramazzotti in a mixing glass filled with ice. Stir to chill and strain into a pre-chilled cocktail glass. Garnish with the orange peel spiral.

*Carve a spiral peel continuously around the whole of the orange with a channel knife (makes about a 1/4 inch groove cut) to make one long strip, taking as little pith as possible.

Yield: 1 drink

THE SOUTHSIDE
SASHA PETRASKE
THE LAMBS CLUB, NEW YORK, NY

During Prohibition, Al Capone complained: "When I sell liquor, they call it bootlegging. When my patrons serve it on silver trays on Lake Shore Drive, they call it hospitality." To mask the awful taste of bootleg gin in the speakeasies of Chicago's South Side, bartenders mixed the swill with lots of sugar and citrus, creating a drink that was named for the neighborhood. Mr. Petraske revamps the original with mint leaves to perfume the yin and yang of simple syrup and lime, transforming the confection into an aromatic and well-balanced gem. A familiar drink made fresh in the execution.

Ingredients:

6 fresh mint leaves (plus 1 leaf for garnish)
3/4 ounce 2:1 simple syrup
3/4 ounce fresh-squeezed lime juice
2 ounces gin

Method:

Add 6 mint leaves, simple syrup, and lime juice into a mixing glass. Muddle the mixture just enough to release the oils of the mint. Add the gin and 4 large ice cubes. Shake vigorously and double strain into a pre-chilled coupe. Garnish with a single fresh mint leaf.

Yield: 1 drink

ULTIMATE GIN & TONIC

LUCAS PAYA
THE BAZAAR BY JOSÉ ANDRÉS, BEVERLY HILLS, CA

Forget aromatherapy. Mr. Paya's marriage of gin and tonic water is a therapeutic experience, the two primary ingredients festooned with a salad of fragrant garnishes, lifting the ubiquitous thirst-quencher to its full potential. Green notes of gin are complimented by the bitterness of quinine in a recommended ratio that varies from 1-to-1 to 1-to-3, served on the side to accommodate personal preference. Use one big chunk of ice; small chips melt too fast and water down the cocktail.

Ingredients:

1 large ice cube (2 1/2-inches)
lemon peel, cut into a 4-inch strip
1 thin lime wheel
3 juniper berries
1 sprig lemon verbena
1 whole edible flower (pestle removed)
2 ounces gin
1 bottle (6.8-ounces) Fever Tree Tonic Water

Method:

Add the ice cube to a highball glass. Twist the lemon peel over the ice to release oils, then wipe rind around rim and drop into the glass. Add a wheel of lime, juniper berries, lemon verbena, and edible flower to the glass. Pour gin over the ice and add tonic water to taste.

Yield: 1 drink

SANTA MONICA GIMLET
VINCENZO MARIANELLA
COPA D'ORO, SANTA MONICA, CA

In Raymond Chandler's *The Long Goodbye*, hard-drinking private eye Philip Marlowe explains that a Gimlet must always be made with Rose's Lime Juice. Don't tell that to the rebellious Mr. Marianella, who shifts the dynamic of the classic cocktail with juices of lemon, cucumber, and celery, perfumed with notes of lychee fruit and elderflowers. The adventurous palate is rewarded with a cuisine-driven formula that capitalizes on local fruit and vegetables.

Ingredients:

2 ounces gin
1/2 to 3/4 ounce cucumber/celery juice*
3/4 ounce St. Germain Elderflower Liqueur
3/4 ounce fresh-squeezed lemon juice
1/4 ounce 2:1 simple syrup
cucumber, sliced into ribbon, for garnish

Method:

Combine gin, cucumber/celery juice, elderflower liqueur, lemon juice, and simple syrup with ice in a shaker. Shake vigorously and strain into a pre-chilled cocktail glass. Garnish with the cucumber ribbon impaled on a stick.

*Wash 1 small cucumber and 1 stalk of celery (keep leaves on), and cut to fit your juicer. Juice, add a pinch of salt, and refrigerate until ready to use.

Yield: 1 drink

AROMATIC #2
VINCENZO MARIANELLA
COPA D'ORO, SANTA MONICA, CA

The swagger of gin is never undermined in Mr. Marianella's cocktail formula. Rather, the spirit's aromatic complexity is reinforced with the artichoke/herbal bouquet of Cynar, vanilla/anise and citrus fragrance of Galliano, and vegetal/bitter incense of celery and rhubarb. Don't forget to express the oils from the grapefruit peel. According to the barkeep, this seemingly subtle detail has a profound effect.

Ingredients:

2 ounces gin
1/2 ounce Galliano
3 teaspoons Cynar
1 dash Bitter Truth Celery Bitters
2 dashes Fee Brothers Rhubarb Bitters
grapefruit peel medallion

Method:

Combine the gin, Galliano, Cynar, and bitters in a mixing glass filled with ice. Stir to chill and strain into a pre-chilled cocktail glass. Squeeze grapefruit peel over surface to express oils and drop into the cocktail.

Yield: 1 drink

THE MARQUEE

JIM ROMDALL
VESSEL, SEATTLE, WA

Although inspired by the re-opening of the 1920s-era movie palace next door to Vessel, Mr. Romdall's cocktail is not overburdened with showiness. Bracing, bitter/sweet flavors of Aperol surround the botanical characters of the gin, partnership tamed with hints of sweetened lemon and woodsy sage. "My style of making cocktails has evolved a bit, keeping the drink very close to the original spirit," confides the drink-smith, "so in this case the gin comes through."

Ingredients:

2 fresh sage leaves (plus 1 leaf for garnish)
3/4 ounce fresh-squeezed lemon juice
1/4 ounce 2:1 simple syrup
1 pinch salt
1 1/2 ounces gin
1/2 ounce Aperol

Method:

Add 2 sage leaves, lemon juice, simple syrup, and salt into a mixing glass. Muddle, gently, until the mixture is pulpy and fragrant. Add gin, Aperol, and ice cubes. Shake vigorously and double strain into a pre-chilled cocktail glass. Float a sage leaf over the drink.

Yield: 1 drink

APPLE PRESS
ALEXEI BERATIS
TOWNE STOVE & SPIRITS, BOSTON, MA

Think of Mr. Beratis as an imaginative matchmaker. He has a gift for pairing ingredients in a way that brings out the best in them and makes them more appealing in a cocktail mosaic than they ever were as loners. The nexus of gin and apple cider, tweaked with elderflower liqueur, is an autumnal twist on the everyday Apple Martini. Its golden color is enhanced with a pretty, ruby-red Dolgo crabapple garnish. Of course, if Dolgos are nowhere to be found, any tiny red apple — or a slice dipped in lemon juice — will do.

Ingredients:

1 1/2 ounces gin
1 1/2 ounces heirloom apple cider
1/2 ounce St. Germain Elderflower Liqueur
Dolgo or other crabapple, for garnish

Method:

Combine gin, apple cider, and elderflower liqueur with ice in a shaker. Shake vigorously and strain into a pre-chilled cocktail glass. Garnish with the crabapple on a skewer.

Yield: 1 drink

COQUETTE
CHRISTY POPE
CUFFS & BUTTONS, BROOKLYN, NY

According to English poet Lord Lytton, "Imitation, if noble and general, insures the best hope of originality." Strawberries found life outside the kitchen in 1922, when the Duke of Manchester introduced the Bloodhound cocktail to America; Maraschino liqueur and citrus juice partnered with gin in bartender Hugo Ensslin's Aviation cocktail, developed at New York's Hotel Wallick. Ms. Pope explores a kinship between the two vintage cocktails, and in the process, breaks new ground.

Ingredients:

2 large strawberries (plus 1 for garnish)
3/4 ounce fresh-squeezed lime juice
1/2 ounce clover honey syrup (2 parts honey, 1 part water)
2 ounces gin
1/4 ounce Luxardo Maraschino liqueur

Method:

Add 2 strawberries, lime juice, and honey syrup into a mixing glass. Muddle, gently, until the mixture is pulpy and fragrant. Add gin, Maraschino liqueur, and ice cubes. Shake vigorously and double strain into a pre-chilled coupe. Garnish with a partially-sliced strawberry on the rim of the glass.

Yield: 1 drink

GIN & JUICE
BRETT FEORE
APIARY RESTAURANT, NEW YORK, NY

Well-honed sensibilities inspire Mr. Feore's calculated risk, as he assembles three robust spirits in perfect equilibrium, each ingredient full of life and flavor. The refreshing and thought-provoking mélange includes tropical fruit, herbal bitters, and botanical-rich gin. A measure of citrus provides "check and balance," and although elderflower liqueur makes only a brief appearance, it leaves behind a beautifully floral fragrance.

Ingredients:

2 teaspoons St. Germain Elderflower Liqueur, for rinse
1 ounce gin
1 ounce VeeV Acai Berry Liquor
1 ounce Aperol
1/2 ounce fresh-squeezed blood orange juice
1/2 ounce fresh-squeezed lime juice
orange peel medallion

Method:

Pour the elderflower liqueur into a Martini glass and swirl it around to coat the glass; pour out any excess. Combine the gin, acai liqueur, Aperol, orange juice, and lime juice with ice in a shaker. Shake vigorously and double strain into the prepared glass. Squeeze orange peel over surface to express oils and drop into the cocktail.

Yield: 1 drink

MEXICAN GIN & TONIC
JOSÉ ANDRÉS
OYAMEL COCINA MEXICANA, WASHINGTON, DC

The trick to presenting a very familiar drink is to make us see it as if for the first time. In the highly distinctive culinary universe of José Andrés, the two ingredients are bound together with aromatic elderflower liqueur, and in place of customary lime, a garden of condiments from the Mexican kitchen. Balancing the bitterness of tonic against the juniper and other flavors in the gin is a matter of taste, so the chef insists on a fresh, individual bottle of tonic with each serving. Brands are a matter of preference, though Mr. Andrés is partial to Fever Tree.

Ingredients:

1 oversized ice cube
1 1/2 ounces gin
1/2 ounce St. Germain Elderflower Liqueur
cilantro leaf, for garnish
3 epazote leaves, for garnish
1 squash blossom, for garnish
1 bottle (6.8-ounces) Fever Tree Tonic Water

Method:

Place the ice cube in a pre-chilled rocks glass. Add the gin and elderflower liqueur. Garnish with cilantro, epazote and squash blossom. Serve with the bottle of tonic on the side.

Yield: 1 drink

THE THYME TRAVELER
HARMONY FRAGA
FARMER BROWN, SAN FRANCISCO, CA

Thyme is a spice rich in both flavor and history. The ancient Romans used thyme as a complement to cheeses and a flavoring for alcoholic beverages. Immensely fragrant and appetizing, thyme provides the herbaceous centerpiece in a culinary cocktail that adds fruit/vegetal complexity to the botanicals of gin. The result is a wondrously fresh, palate-cleansing drink that turns cocktail hour into an occasion.

Ingredients:

4 to 5 fresh thyme leaves
3 mint leaves
2 slices cucumber (plus 1 slice for garnish)
1/2 ounce 2:1 simple syrup
1/2 ounce fresh-squeezed lemon juice
splash fresh pineapple juice
1 1/2 ounces gin

Method:

Add thyme leaves, mint leaves, 2 cucumber slices, simple syrup, lemon juice, and pineapple juice into a mixing glass. Muddle, gently, until the mixture is pulpy and fragrant. Add gin and ice cubes. Shake vigorously and double strain into a pre-chilled Martini glass. Garnish with a cucumber slice on the rim of the glass.

Yield: 1 drink

BRING THE BEET BACK
HARMONY FRAGA
FARMER BROWN, SAN FRANCISCO, CA

So much is attempted here. The complex interplay of savory and fruit flavors makes for a marvelous, multilayered experience — a cocktail that is almost good for you. Beets are clearly the prevailing personalities of the work, giving all they can give to the gin without mugging the juniper. Berry, citrus, and jammy components take hold, racing across the tongue.

Ingredients:

2 blackberries
1/2 ounce blackberry or mixed berry juice
1/2 ounce fresh-squeezed orange juice
1/4 ounce fresh-squeezed lemon juice
1 teaspoon kumquat jam*
1 1/2 ounces beet-infused gin**
1 small kumquat, for garnish

Method:

Add blackberries, berry juice, orange juice, lemon juice, and kumquat jam into a mixing glass. Muddle, gently, until the mixture is pulpy and fragrant. Add gin and ice cubes. Shake vigorously and double strain into a pre-chilled cocktail glass. Garnish with kumquat on a skewer.

*Peel and quarter 2 cups of fresh kumquats and warm in a small saucepan over medium heat. Reduce heat and add 1 cup of sugar. Mix to combine. Add 2 tablespoons of water and 2 tablespoons of orange juice. Keep on reduced/low heat for 8 to 10 minutes, stirring until mixture thickens. Remove from heat and refrigerate until ready to use.

**Peel and slice 1 large or 2 small beets. Place in a large pitcher or other container with a lid. Add the contents of a 1-liter bottle of gin and stir. Cover and keep in a cool, dark room for 3 to 5 days, stirring once per day. Strain and rebottle.

Yield: 1 drink

CEDAR FEVER
BILL NORRIS
FINO RESTAURANT PATIO & BAR, AUSTIN, TX

Needless to say, juniper is the dominant botanical in Old Tom-style gin, so it's no accident when Mr. Norris exaggerates his cocktail's assertive character with similar flavoring from a cousin to the juniper. Something of an oddity, Zirbenz Austrian Stone Pine Liqueur is made from the fruit of what becomes a pine cone, harvested in the high Alps. Besides a rush of floral pine, the formula displays notes of blueberry, mountain rose and a hint of peppery reed grass.

Ingredients:

2 ounces gin
1/2 ounce St. Germain Elderflower Liqueur
1/2 ounce Zirbenz Austrian Stone Pine Liqueur
spritz Peychaud's bitters, for aromatics
lemon peel medallion

Method:

Combine the gin, elderflower liqueur, and pine liqueur in a mixing glass filled with ice. Stir to chill and strain into a pre-chilled cocktail glass. Spritz bitters over top from an atomizer. Squeeze lemon peel over surface to express oils and drop into the cocktail.

Yield: 1 drink

BROTHERLY LOVE

JOSH LOVING
FINO RESTAURANT PATIO & BAR, AUSTIN, TX

Balance in a cocktail is achieved when individual components are seamlessly combined into a single experience. As you "drop in" for your first sip of Mr. Loving's medley, you taste something that is wonderfully complex and yet harmonious at the same time. Herbal, floral, fruity, winey, and spicy notes hit the palate in different, distinguishable waves, punctuated with bitter/citrus aromatics, all skillfully building upon the base of gin.

Ingredients:

1 1/4 ounces gin
3/4 ounce Cocchi Americano Aperitivo Bianco
1/2 ounce St-Germain Elderflower Liqueur
1/2 ounce Domaine de Canton Ginger Liqueur
3 dashes orange bitters
orange peel medallion

Method:

Combine the gin, Aperitivo Bianco, elderflower liqueur, ginger liqueur, and orange bitters in a mixing glass filled with ice. Stir to chill and strain into a pre-chilled cocktail glass. Squeeze orange peel over surface to express oils and drop into the cocktail.

Yield: 1 drink

THE SAKURANBO
JIM ROMDALL
VESSEL, SEATTLE, WA

Japanese cherry blossoms, called sakuranbo, provide leitmotif for Mr. Romdall's composition, as he employs cherry and bitter-almond flavors of kirschwasser as counterpoint to the Martini-informed partnership of gin and Lillet. To complete his full-dress treatment, the barman muddles fresh rhubarb, giving weight and lending deep, piquant flavor.

Ingredients:

1-inch piece fresh rhubarb
3/4 ounce fresh-squeezed lemon juice
1/4 ounce 2:1 simple syrup
1 1/2 ounces gin
1/2 ounce Clear Creek Kirschwasser
1/2 ounce Lillet blanc
1 mint leaf, for garnish

Method:

Add the rhubarb, lemon juice, and simple syrup into a mixing glass. Muddle, gently, until the mixture is pulpy and fragrant. Add gin, kirschwasser, Lillet, and ice cubes. Shake vigorously and double strain into a pre-chilled cocktail glass. Garnish with spanked mint leaf.

Yield: 1 drink

OLD TOM'S APPLE
TIM KOSUGE
ARAKA, CLAYTON, MO

Inveterate Martini drinker Noel Coward once advised, "Trust your instincts. If you have no instincts, trust your impulses." Tapping his own
creative impulses, Mr. Kosuge builds upon the foundation of gin and
vermouth with a savory blend of apple juice and balsamic vinegar, fine-
tuned with the citrus juice of a lemon. Slowly, the characters of an Old
Tom-style gin emerge, as if breaking free from a powerful construct.
There is a harmony among flavors, and it all makes for a comforting
nightcap.

Ingredients:

1 1/2 ounces gin
1/2 ounce dry vermouth
1/2 ounce white balsamic-brown sugar reduction*
1 ounce fresh apple juice (green apple preferred)
1/8 ounce fresh-squeezed lemon juice
cinnamon-dusted apple wheel, for garnish

Method:

Combine the gin, vermouth, balsamic reduction, apple juice, and lemon
juice in a mixing glass filled with ice. Stir to chill and double strain into
a pre-chilled cocktail glass. With a mandolin, slice a very thin apple
wheel. Dust with ground cinnamon and float over the drink.

*In a small sauce pan over medium heat, add 1/2 cup white balsamic
vinegar. Once the vinegar is hot enough to dissolve sugar, add 2 teaspoons of brown sugar. Stir continuously with a wooden spoon, allowing the mixture to simmer and the vinegar to evaporate. Remove from
heat about one minute after adding the sugar and taste. If the vinegar
is still too strong, continue to heat, tasting until you find the right
flavor and consistency.

Yield: 1 drink

FRENCH 78
TIM KOSUGE
ARAKA, CLAYTON, MO

The original incarnation of this cocktail is attributed to American soldiers in Paris during World War I. They added gin to Champagne to crank up its potency and christened the intoxicant after an artillery gun that rattled 75-millimeter shells at the Germans (at a rate of 30 rounds a minute). Mr. Kosuge's update of the "French 75" still packs a wallop, but perfumed with floral liqueurs, the drink is more stylish and accessible than ever.

Ingredients:

1 1/2 ounces gin
1/4 ounce Rothman & Winter Creme de Violette
1/4 ounce St. Germain Elderflower Liqueur
1/4 ounce fresh-squeezed lemon juice
Champagne (or dry sparkling wine), to top up
lemon peel, spiral-cut, for garnish*

Method:

Combine the gin, Crème de Violette, elderflower liqueur, and lemon juice with ice in a shaker. Shake vigorously and double strain into a pre-chilled coupe. Top up with the Champagne and garnish with the lemon spiral.

*Cut a thin piece of lemon peel with a v-shaped channel knife. Coil the peel around a straw or chopstick, and place in a glass of water in the freezer for 15 minutes.

Yield: 1 drink

PATTAYA GO GO
CHAD SOLOMON
CUFFS & BUTTONS, BROOKLYN, NY

Balance and detail are important elements in Mr. Solomon's homage to Thai cuisine, a style known for combining ingredients at opposite ends of the flavor spectrum. The infusion of lemon myrtle tea leaves imparts tropical, lemony flavors to the gin, while lime juice adds lively, floral acidity. Savory bouquet of sage and citrus wrap around the sweet, creamy coconut syrup courtesy of zesty cilantro, with heat from the Serrano pepper lingering around the edges. This drink transcends the cocktail hour and finds harmony with foods on the table.

Ingredients:

2 sprigs cilantro
1 thin slice Serrano pepper
3/4 ounce Torani Coconut Syrup
3/4 ounce fresh-squeezed lime juice
2 ounces lemon myrtle-infused gin*
1 purple orchid, for garnish
pinch, fresh-grated ginger, for garnish

Method:

Add the cilantro, pepper, coconut syrup, and lime juice into a mixing glass. Muddle, gently, until the mixture is pulpy and fragrant. Add infused gin and ice cubes. Shake vigorously and double strain into a pre-chilled coupe. Garnish with purple orchid and ginger essence.

*Add 1 tablespoon of lemon myrtle tea into 1 cup of gin. Let stand at room temperature for 1 hour. Strain off tea (do not push down on solids while straining). Place in capped bottle, and store in refrigerator until ready to use.

Yield: 1 drink

LEFT OF BEAUTIFUL
ANDREW FRIEDMAN
LIBERTY BAR, SEATTLE, WA

The beauty of Mr. Friedman's cocktail is the way in which a more sophisticated French cousin to simple syrup, the gastrique, adds a burst of flavor. The term refers to the syrupy "sauce" formed by reducing a combination of wine vinegar, sugar, and fruit — in this case fresh lemon juice. He doubles down on the lemony note with a lemon verbena infusion, bringing citrus to the forefront of gin's flavor profile, while still retaining classic notes of juniper berries. The result is a crowd-pleasing combination that has sweetness, texture, and a slightly pungent component, with less subtlety, more muscle.

Ingredients:

2 ounces lemon verbena-infused gin*
1/4 ounce lemon gastrique**
2 dashes Peychaud's bitters
lemon peel, cut into a long spiral, for garnish

Method:

Combine the infused gin, lemon gastrique, and bitters in a mixing glass filled with ice. Stir to chill and strain into a rocks glass over 1 large ice cube. Rub the lemon peel around the rim of the glass, then drop into the cocktail.

*Add 2 handfuls of rinsed, fresh lemon verbena to the contents of a 750-ml bottle of gin in a large pitcher or other container with a lid. Infuse for 1 to 3 days (according to taste), then strain through a coffee filter and rebottle.

** Combine 5 ounces of water and 3 ounces of fresh-squeezed lemon juice in a small sauce pan over medium heat. Simmer until liquid is reduced by half, then add 2 ounces of sugar and a pinch of salt; stir to mix. Off the heat, carefully stir in 1 ounce of champagne wine vinegar and let steep for 20 minutes. Strain into an airtight container and let cool completely, then refrigerate until ready to use.

Yield: 1 drink

WEAPON OF CHOICE
STEFAN RAVALLI
BARNDIVA, HEALDSBURG, CA

Always the provocateur, Mr. Ravalli amplifies gin with the unapologetic infusion of pungent bay leaves and Serrano pepper (said to be 5 times hotter than the jalapeño). Herbal, spice, and citrus elements dance with botanicals, bitters, and heat in his idiosyncratic culinary landscape. This drink is a real find and well worth the complexity level of an attempt. Notes from the drinksmith: Cock and Bull brand, a spicier ginger beer, is preferred; adjust lime juice as needed to balance the sweetness of the ginger beer.

Ingredients:

3/4 ounce bay leaf-and-Serrano pepper-infused gin*
1 1/2 ounces Pimm's
1 1/4 ounces watermelon-lemongrass puree**
1/4 to 1/2 ounce fresh-squeezed lime juice
Cock and Bull Ginger Beer, to top up
1 cucumber slice, for garnish
1 whole bay leaf, for garnish
1 watermelon slice, for garnish

Method:

Combine infused gin, Pimm's, watermelon-lemongrass puree, and lime juice with ice in a shaker. Shake vigorously and double strain into a Collins glass filled with ice. Top up with ginger beer. Garnish with bay leaf, watermelon slice, and cucumber slice.

*Add 6 bay leaves and a small slice of Serrano pepper to the contents of a 750-ml bottle of gin in a large pitcher or other container with a lid. Allow ingredients to steep for 2 hours; strain gently (do not press the leaves to extract excess gin) and rebottle.

**Clean and coarsely cube 1/2-pound of watermelon. Combine with 1 stalk of lemongrass and blend to puree.

Yield: 1 drink

STEVE-O'S TUXEDO
STEVE SCHNEIDER
EMPLOYEES ONLY, NEW YORK, NY

It's the latest evocation of a drink that goes far back into cocktail lore. The White Lady (also known as a Delilah, Chelsea Sidecar or Lillian Forever) has been evolving ever since 1919, when Harry MacElhone introduced the formula at Ciro's Club in London. Mr. Schneider's gin-forward adaptation finds its orange notes in bitters and zest rather than Cointreau. The resulting drink is a light, refreshing, yet still brisk rendition of the classic.

Ingredients:

1 3/4 ounces gin
1 egg white
1/2 ounce 2:1 simple syrup
3/4 ounce fresh-squeezed lemon juice
2 dashes orange bitters
orange peel medallion

Method:

Combine the gin, egg white, simple syrup, lemon juice, and orange bitters with ice in a shaker. Shake vigorously and strain into a pre-chilled cocktail glass. Squeeze orange peel over surface to express oils and drop into the cocktail.

Yield: 1 drink

# QUEEN ELEANOR
BRANDON JOSIE
15 ROMOLO, SAN FRANCISCO, CA

Eleanor of Aquitaine was portrayed by Katherine Hepburn in *The Lion in Winter*, interesting, since each woman defined her time by being ahead of it. As the ubiquitous and persistent Appletini proves, the Martini prototype can become a showcase for favorite fruit flavors. In his progressive interpretation, Mr. Josie brightens the prominent botanicals of gin with herbal vermouth and sweet, aromatic peach liqueur. A drop of vegetal bitters makes it *l'affaire du coeur* at first sip.

Ingredients:

1 1/2 ounces gin
1/2 ounce dry vermouth
1/2 ounce Creme De Peche
1 dash celery bitters
fennel frond, for garnish

Method:

Combine the gin, vermouth, peach liqueur, and bitters in a mixing glass filled with ice. Stir to chill and strain into a pre-chilled cocktail glass. Garnish with the fennel frond.

Yield: 1 drink

GROUNDS FOR DIVORCE
TREVOR EASTER
RICKHOUSE, SAN FRANCISCO, CA

He provokes the breakup of a long-standing relationship. Moving on from the tried and true Gin Sour formula, Mr. Easter's infidelity begins by replacing lemon with lime (in the direction of F. Scott Fitzgerald's Gin Rickey), and plain sugar with herbal-infused sweeteners. After hard shaking to aerate with egg white and scenting with bitters, the liberated construct is topped up with chilled sparkling wine rather than club soda. A tender mint leaf provides an enchanting scent, right under the drinker's nose.

Ingredients:

6 fresh mint leaves (plus 1 leaf for garnish)
3/4 ounce fresh-squeezed lime juice
1/2 ounce lavender honey*
1/2 ounce turbinado 2:1 simple syrup
1/2 ounce egg white
1 1/2 ounces gin
sparkling wine, chilled, to top up
spritz Angostura bitters, for aromatics

Method:

Add 6 mint leaves, lime juice, lavender honey, simple syrup, and egg white into a mixing glass. Muddle, gently, until the mixture is pulpy and fragrant. Add gin and ice cubes. Shake vigorously and double strain into a pre-chilled coupe. Top up with a splash of sparkling wine. Spritz bitters over top from an atomizer, and garnish with mint leaf.

*Combine 1 cup organic honey, 1 cup water, and 1 cup lavender blossoms in medium saucepan over medium heat. Stir regularly and remove from heat once the honey and water have bonded. Strain out the lavender and chill the syrup until ready to use.

Yield: 1 drink

NOIR 75

JENNIFER EMBLETON
SKOOL, SAN FRANCISCO, CA

New York's Stork Club was the epitome of American glamour in the 1940s and 50s, catering to the rich and famous of show business, sports, politics, and the underworld. It was at the legendary nightclub where the French 75 was, according to Lucius Beebe (author of *The Stork Club Bar Book*), "enshrined in the pharmacopoeia of alcohol artistry." Inspired by a genre of black-and-white films with hard-drinking heroes and femmes fatale, Ms. Embleton heightens the shadows with blackberry syrup while allowing gin and sparkling wine to remain central characters.

Ingredients:

1 ounce gin
1/2 ounce fresh-squeezed lemon juice
3/4 ounce Torani Blackberry Syrup
Prosecco, to top up

Method:

Place a Champagne flute in the freezer and chill at least 2 hours. Combine the gin, lemon juice, and blackberry syrup with ice in a shaker. Shake vigorously, then double strain into the pre-chilled flute. Top up with the Prosecco. Serve without garnish.

Yield: 1 drink

THE COMMUNIST
ERIC TRICHON
MERCATO BAR AND KITCHEN, ITHACA, NY

Communism is identified with the color red for "blood of the workers," symbolizing the suffering of the proletariat, and inspiring a vintage cocktail formula. Like tenets of a manifesto, the ingredients in the red-hued cocktail add up to a full, fresh restorative, updated for all social classes, and stirred until as cold as Mother Russia. Savory black cherry essence of Cherry Heering mingles easily with the citrus juices, building a bridge to the herbal notes of the gin. To your health, comrade!

Ingredients:

1 ounce gin
1/2 ounce Cherry Heering
1 ounce fresh-squeezed orange juice
3/4 ounce fresh-squeezed lemon juice

Method:

Combine the gin, Cherry Heering, and fruit juices in a mixing glass filled with ice. Stir to chill and double strain into a pre-chilled Martini glass. Serve without garnish.

Yield: 1 drink

Sources and Resources

Ingredients and supplies called for in recipes can be found at:
www.alltheginjoints.com

Bartenders on Duty

Ahlo, Keenan, **BOKA Kitchen + Bar**, Seattle, WA

Andrés, José, **Zaytinya**, Washington, DC

Andrews, Ryan, **Liege**, Oakland, CA

Bates, Zahra, **Providence**, Los Angeles, CA

Bayha, Dan, **The Foundry on Melrose**, Los Angeles, CA

Beratis, Alexei, **Towne Stove & Spirits**, Boston, MA

Bernbach, Adam, **Proof**, Washington, DC

Bertani, Aimee, **The Gilt Club**, Portland OR

Bonasera, Sonny, **Villains Tavern**, Los Angeles, CA

Brown, Derek, **The Columbia Room at Passenger**, Washington, DC

Cannon, Jackson, **Eastern Standard**, Boston, MA

Carre, Ray, **OM Restaurant and Lounge**, Cambridge, MA

Casey, Muzlina, **Cure Bar and Bistro**, Washington, DC

Clements, Brandon, **Spruce**, San Francisco, CA

D'Amato-Moran, Victoria, **Cent'Anni Cocktails**, San Francisco, CA

DeGroot, Bill, **Quiessence**, Phoenix, AZ

Evans, Scott, **Pago**, Salt Lake City, UT

Feore, Brett, **Apiary Restaurant**, New York, NY

Fraga, Harmony, **Farmer Brown**, San Francisco, CA

Frankel, Christopher, **Anvil Bar & Refuge**, Houston, TX

Frey, Erika, **Cyrus**, Healdsburg, CA

Friedman, Andrew, **Liberty Bar,** Seattle, WA

Goad, James, **Slow Club**, San Francisco, CA

Golden, Ryan, **Plan B Bar + Kitchen**, Chicago, IL

Gonzales, Dominique, **Zocalo**, Sacramento, CA

Hanson, Pip, **Cafe Maude**, Minneapolis, MN

Heugel, Bobby, **Anvil Bar & Refuge**, Houston, TX

Houghtaling, Leah, **Felicia's Atomic Lounge**, Ithaca, NY

Joly, Charles, **The Drawing Room**, Chicago, IL

Kosmas, Jason, **Employees Only**, New York, NY

Kosuge, Tim, **Araka**, Clayton, MO

Krueger, Rob, **Employees Only**, New York, NY

Kupitz, Ross, **Damico Kitchen**, Minneapolis, MN

Landers, Rodney, **Blue Bar at the Algonquin Hotel**, New York, NY

Lilly, Aleko, **Barrio Capitol Hill**, Seattle, WA

Lotz, Ryan, **Lineage**, Brookline, MA

Loving, Josh, **FINO Restaurant Patio & Bar**, Austin, TX

Magondi, Sashu, **OM Restaurant and Lounge**, Cambridge, MA

Marianella, Vincenzo, **Copa D'Oro**, Santa Monica, CA

McGee, Paul, **The Whistler**, Chicago, IL

McKinley, Luke, **Ravish**, Seattle, WA

Minchow, Andy, **Holeman and Finch Public House**, Atlanta, GA

Moo, David, **Quarter Bar**, Brooklyn, NY

Morgenthaler, Jeffrey, **Clyde Common**, Portland, OR

Norris, Bill, **FINO Restaurant Patio & Bar**, Austin, TX

Paya, Lucas, **The Bazaar by José Andrés**, Beverly Hills, CA

Peek, Debbi, **The Bristol**, Chicago, IL

Petraske, Sasha, **The Lambs Club**, New York, NY

Pope, Christy, **Cuffs & Buttons**, Brooklyn, NY

Rademacher, Josh, **Trinity and the Pope**, Asbury Park, NJ

Ravalli, Stefan, **Barndiva**, Healdsburg, CA

Reiner, Julie, **Clover Club**, Brooklyn, NY

Reissmueller, Lydia, **Tender Bar**, Portland, OR

Richtmyer, Jennifer, **Grange Kitchen & Bar**, Ann Arbor, MI

Roberts, Christopher, **Patowmack Farm**, Lovettsville, VA

Robinson, Darryl, **Hudson Bar**, New York, NY

Romdall, Jim, **Vessel**, Seattle, WA

Ryan, Mike, **Sable Kitchen and Bar**, Chicago, IL

Schneider, Steve, **Employees Only**, New York, NY

Seger, Adam, **Nacional 27**, Chicago, IL

Seider, Gregory, **The Summit Bar**, New York, NY

Shapiro, Andrew, **Dino**, Washington, DC

Shearin, Michael, **Drago Centro**, Los Angeles, CA

Shelton, Stephen, **Cin-Cin**, Los Gatos, CA

Solomon, Chad, **Cuffs & Buttons**, Brooklyn, NY

Sprouse, Claire, **Beaver's Icehouse**, Houston, TX

Stoddard, Mark, **The Bitter Bar**, Boulder, CO

Thibodeaux, Sean, **Clever**, New Orleans, LA

Toste, Max, **Deep Ellum**, Allston, MA

Travers, Clif, **Bar Celona**, Brooklyn, NY

Trichon, Eric, **Mercato Bar and Kitchen**, Ithaca, NY
Whitead, Jermaine, **Barrio Capitol Hill**, Seattle, WA
Whitton, David, **Villains Tavern**, Los Angeles, CA
Zaric, Dushan, **Employees Only**, New York, NY
Zvi, Elad, **Bar Lab**, Miami, FL

GINDEX

124

Last Call

Author Michael Turback became a gentlemanly drinker during his tender days at Cornell, and he remained curious and adventurous on the matter of imbibing throughout a prominent career as restaurateur and saloonkeeper.

Cocktail programs developed in his establishments have influenced the beverage business for over three decades. Michael is credited with reviving classic formulas, influencing a generation of "craft bartenders," and elevating mixology to a culinary art.

As an arbiter of food, wine, and cocktails, he continues to advise the hospitality industry. As an author, he has previously taken on, with distinction, such topics as the ice cream sundae, the banana split, hot chocolate, coffee drinks, Finger Lakes wine country, and his hometown farmers market.

To visit Michael Turback online, go to: www.michaelturback.com

— Notes —

— NOTES —

— Notes —

— Notes —

— Notes —

Printed in Great Britain
by Amazon.co.uk, Ltd.,
Marston Gate.